Historical American Biographies

EMILY DICKINSON

Solitary and Celebrated Poet

Amy Paulson Herstek

Enslow Publishers, Inc.

40 Industrial Road   PO Box 38
Box 398   Aldershot
Berkeley Heights, NJ 07922   Hants GU12 6BP
USA   UK

http://www.enslow.com

Library of Congress Cataloging-in-Publication Data

Herstek, Amy Paulson.
    Emily Dickinson : solitary and celebrated poet / Amy Paulson Herstek.
        p. cm. — (Historical American biographies)
    Summary: A biography of the nineteenth-century American poet.
    Includes bibliographical references (p.) and index.
    ISBN 0-7660-1977-2
    1. Dickinson, Emily, 1830-1886—Juvenile literature. 2. Poets,
American—19th century—Biography—Juvenile literature. [1. Dickinson,
Emily, 1830-1886. 2. Poets, American. 3. Women—Biography.] I. Title.
II. Series.
PS1541.Z5 H47   2003
811'.4—dc21

                                        2002153859

Printed in the United States of America

10 9 8 7 6 5 4 3 2 1

To Our Readers:
We have done our best to make sure all Internet Addresses in this book were
active and appropriate when we went to press. However, the author and the publisher have no control over and assume no liability for the material available on
those Internet sites or on other Web sites they may link to. Any comments or sug-
gestions can be sent by e-mail to comments@enslow.com or to the address on the
back cover.

Illustration Credits: Amy Paulson Herstek, pp. 53, 58, 112; ©2003
ArtToday.com, Inc., All Rights Reserved, p. 40; Photo by Frank Ward,
courtesy the Dickinson Homestead and the Trustees of Amherst
College, pp. 100, 106, 109; Courtesy Millicent Todd Bingham, repro-
duced from the *Dictionary of American Portraits*, published by Dover
Publications, Inc., in 1967, p. 8; Engraving by Charles B. Hall, repro-
duced from the *Dictionary of American Portraits*, published by Dover
Publications, Inc., in 1967, p. 73; Enslow Publishers, Inc., p. 14;
Reproduced from the Collections of the Library of Congress, pp. 17, 29,
35, 38, 43, 56, 68, 69, 80, 81, 92, 94, 96; Reproduced from the
Dictionary of American Portraits, published by Dover Publications, Inc.,
in 1967, pp. 4, 77.

Cover Illustration: Photo by Frank Ward, courtesy the Dickinson
Homestead and the Trustees of Amherst College (Background);
Reproduced from the *Dictionary of American Portraits*, published by
Dover Publications, Inc., in 1967 (Dickinson Portrait).

CONTENTS

Emily Dickinson

1

A LITERARY TREASURE

Not long after Emily Dickinson's death in 1886, her younger sister, Lavinia ("Vinnie" to those who knew her well), and sister-in-law, Sue, began to sort through Dickinson's belongings. Stuffed at the bottom of a dresser drawer, they discovered what is often viewed as a literary treasure—nearly a thousand of Dickinson's poems and letters in a mostly jumbled state. Some of the poems were in final form. However, many of them were drafts and included three or four versions of the same poem. It would take hours to sort through the trunk that the letters and poems were in, and years before any of the poems would be published.

Before she died, Dickinson began grouping the poems into fascicles, little books of five or six pages apiece. Lavinia and Sue found forty such booklets. There were many notes and jottings. It was as if Emily Dickinson had written down every thought she had about nature, life, death, eternity, love, and life in Amherst, Massachusetts. It was in this town that the Dickinsons were a prominent, but not always happy, family.

Dickinson's family was aware that she wrote, but they were shocked to find so many poems. Only Sue Dickinson, the wife of Dickinson's older brother, Austin, had ever read any of her work. Lavinia was completely surprised to find so many letters and poems, including scores of elegies—poems written to express sorrow about a person who had died.

Over the years, Dickinson mostly stayed at home in the house on Main Street in Amherst. She went out less and less over the years, and rarely saw people when they came to visit her. Because she preferred being alone to the company of friends, she communicated with people through notes and letters. Correspondence was an extremely large part of Dickinson's life and she frequently included poems in her letters to friends and family. Writing was the way she kept in touch with the world.

Dickinson was unsure about publishing her poems during her lifetime. She once had said that she did not believe it was proper for a woman to publish, and that doing so would make her too vulnerable to public criticism. "I would as soon undress in public, as to give my poems to the world," she had once said.[1] Publishing her poems might have made her feel like her private life was exposed. But Lavinia Dickinson was completely dedicated to the task of publishing her sister's poems. In fact, if it was not for Lavinia Dickinson's extreme dedication, people might not know of Emily Dickinson and her writing today.

Lavinia initially decided that Sue Dickinson should go through everything and edit the poems so they could be published. After all, Sue and Emily had been close friends for more than forty years. Many of the notes and poems were written to or about Sue. So Sue began to work on them. But after two years, Lavinia asked for them back. Perhaps she thought Sue was taking too long with them, or maybe she was afraid Sue would not delete negative references to the Dickinson family. No one really knows for sure.

Lavinia then assigned the task to Mabel Loomis Todd, an Amherst neighbor who also believed in Dickinson's talent as a writer. She loved nature almost as much as Dickinson had, and was a close friend of the family. Todd spent countless hours sorting through the poems, transcribing, editing, and

After Emily Dickinson's death, her friend Mabel Loomis Todd (pictured) helped get her poetry published.

trying to put dates on them. Very few of the poems and letters were dated. Only twenty-four of them had titles. Todd collaborated with Lavinia and her brother, Austin. They examined Dickinson's handwriting over the years and analyzed how it changed, in order to put approximate dates on the poems. Some of the difficulties with dating or putting Dickinson's letters and poems in chronological order were enhanced by her family's desire to convey a certain image of their sister, or to portray themselves more favorably. They tried to conceal conflicts in their own relationships that Dickinson wrote about in her poems.

What would Dickinson have thought about all of this attention to her writing? We do not know for sure, but she had instructed Lavinia to burn all her letters after her death. This was a common practice at the time. Dickinson rarely published her poetry during her lifetime. Only about ten of Dickinson's poems were published while she was alive.

Mabel Todd and Lavinia Dickinson took three years to edit several hundred poems. Once the poems were edited, Lavinia had Todd categorize them into sections entitled "Life," "Love," "Nature," "Time," and "Eternity." Todd then took them to Thomas Wentworth Higginson, a scholar in Boston. Todd traveled from Amherst to Boston in November 1889 to discuss the possibility of publishing them. Initially, Higginson was skeptical of the idea. Dickinson had sent him some poems thirty years earlier, and he did not believe then that they should be published.

However, when Todd showed him a stack of her personal favorites, Higginson was astonished at their beauty and asked her to send all of the poems to him so he could read them. After several months, Higginson said that Dickinson's poems were impressive. However, he remained hesitant to publish them because they were written so differently from other poetry that was popular at the time. Dickinson's poems seldom rhymed. She put in strange punctuation. Some of her poems were difficult to understand. While he had them, Higginson recategorized the poems he read and even gave them titles in instances where Dickinson chose not to do so.

Todd found Higginson's reluctance to publish the poems frustrating, but she realized she would need his support. Higginson took the poems to Houghton Mifflin, a publishing house where he worked. He was told the poems were odd and that "the rhymes were all wrong."[2] So he suggested another publishing company, Roberts Brothers. At one time, Dickinson had sent some of her poems to Roberts Brothers. But there, too, the publishers were not willing to take a chance on Dickinson's poems. "It has always seemed to me that it would be unwise to perpetuate Miss Dickinson's poems," publisher Thomas Niles of Roberts Brothers wrote to Thomas Higginson in the summer of 1890. "They are quite as remarkable for defects as for beauties & are generally devoid of true poetical qualities," Niles said.[3] Todd and Lavinia persisted, and Niles finally agreed to publish five hundred copies of a book of Dickinson's poems.

In his preface to the first edition of poems, Higginson sought to prepare readers for Dickinson's unconventional verse. He wrote that she was a daring writer, who wrote "without the thought of publication, and solely by way of expression of the writer's own mind."[4] Emily Dickinson's poems, Higginson forewarned, "will seem to the reader like poetry torn up by the roots, with rain and dew and earth still clinging to them, giving a freshness and a fragrance not otherwise to be conveyed."[5]

Higginson did more than introduce readers to Dickinson's poetry; he put onto the printed page that which the people of Amherst had whispered about for nearly three decades. He mythologized Emily Elizabeth Dickinson, for better or for worse, as a recluse "as invisible to the world as if she dwelt in a nunnery [a convent]."[6]

By the time she died, Dickinson had stayed within the boundaries of the family's mansion, known as the Homestead, for twenty-five years. When her sister-in-law and close friend Sue Dickinson wrote Dickinson's obituary for the local newspaper, the *Springfield Republican*, she tried to explain Dickinson's desire for solitude by quoting one of Dickinson's favorite poets, Robert Browning. "'The mesh of her soul,' as Browning calls the body, "was too rare," Sue wrote, to allow contact with other people.[7] People in Amherst had speculated for years as to why Dickinson behaved so peculiarly. With the publication of her poems, interest in her life was rekindled.

The first volume of poems was a huge success, much to Higginson's surprise. The public loved Dickinson's poems and their refreshing look at life.

In 1891, Roberts Brothers published a second edition of her poems. This time, Todd provided her insights on Dickinson's life. Todd wrote in the book's introduction that Dickinson touched upon her poetic themes "sometimes lightly, sometimes almost humorously, more often with weird and peculiar power; but she is never by any chance frivolous or trivial."[8] As for Dickinson's withdrawal from society, Todd tried to dispel the myth that Higginson had established. Dickinson had not isolated herself because she was ill or had a broken heart, Todd explained. Instead, Todd said that Dickinson "had tried society and the world, and found them lacking."[9] But Todd only made Dickinson seem more eccentric and mysterious when she wrote:

> Storm, wind, the wild March sky, sunsets and dawns; the birds and bees, butterflies and flowers or her garden, with a few trusted human friends, were sufficient companionship. . . . Immortality was close about her; and while never morbid or melancholy, she lived in its presence.[10]

Todd's words made Dickinson sound like a seldom seen, almost mythical creature.

As a result, the myth of Emily Dickinson grew over the years, along with continuing interest in her poems. Throughout her life, Dickinson appeared to both long for recognition and fear the possible criticism that public exposure might bring her. She did not really write for publication; she wrote because she was fiercely creative. Writing was her way of expressing herself. In one of her own poems, Dickinson foretells how her writing would one day be published—after her death and without her direct input:

> *This is my letter to the world,*
> *That never wrote to me,—*
> *The simple news that Nature told,*
> *With tender majesty.*
>
> *Her message is committed*
> *To hands I cannot see;*
> *For love of her, sweet countrymen,*
> *Judge tenderly of me!*[11]

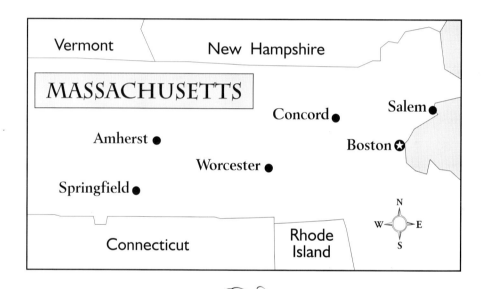

Emily Dickinson spent most of her life in Massachusetts, especially at home in Amherst.

2

THE DICKINSON HERITAGE

Emily Elizabeth Dickinson was born at home in Amherst, Massachusetts, on December 10, 1830. The story goes that Emily's mother, after whom she was named, endured her labor while a workman hung wallpaper in her bedroom.[1] This anecdote might seem a bit unusual, and may not even be true, but it does explain the kind of household into which Emily was born. The Dickinsons possessed New England practicality but also saw the value of lighthearted humor.

One way to understand Emily and how she became such a famous poet is to become acquainted with her family. The Dickinson family was close-knit and had deep roots in the community of Amherst.

Emily's grandfather, Samuel Fowler Dickinson, began his career as a teacher, then became a successful lawyer and leading citizen before he overextended himself financially and lost the family fortune.

Samuel Dickinson married Lucretia Gunn in 1802, and the couple had nine children. Emily's father, Edward Dickinson, was the oldest child. Samuel Dickinson built the family mansion, known as the Homestead, on Main Street. It was said to be the first brick house in Amherst.

Samuel Dickinson strongly believed in the importance of a good education for both girls and boys, and one of his greatest accomplishments was helping to establish the Amherst Academy in 1812. He also was one of the original founders of Amherst College, which was established in 1821. At the time, there was much debate over whether the college should be built in Amherst or in another nearby town. Samuel Dickinson convinced everyone that the college should be built in Amherst. After winning over the local leaders, he persuaded the Massachusetts legislature to grant a charter and provide land for the school. His daughter Lucretia described in a letter to her brother, Edward, who was away at school, how Samuel set off for Boston: "Father left in the yellow gig [carriage] for the Bay Road this morning. He has gone to Boston by coach to see about getting a charter for something they propose to call Amherst College. He looked so fine in his white beaver [hat] and new great coat."[2]

Samuel Dickinson even donated six hundred dollars of his own money and cosigned a fifteen-thousand-dollar bond. Both sums were considerable at the time. As a reward for his generosity, Samuel Dickinson became the first treasurer of Amherst College. It was an honor that would be bestowed on his son, Edward, and later on his grandson, Austin.

But Samuel Dickinson did not succeed in every endeavor. In 1828, he was elected to the

Emily's grandfather helped found Amherst College. The chapel and grounds of the school are pictured.

Massachusetts legislature. However, that same year he unsuccessfully ran for a seat in the U.S. Congress. He also tried to start a law school at Amherst College. By 1832, the college was in financial trouble. In 1833, Samuel Dickinson sold his half of the Homestead and left for Cincinnati, Ohio. Ohio was considered "the West" by New Englanders at the time, and it was a very underdeveloped place. Samuel Dickinson went to work at a school there. He became ill and died in Hudson, Ohio, on April 22, 1838. His personal failings were a source of embarrassment to the rest of the family. Emily was only seven years old at the time of his death.

Emily's Parents: Edward and Emily

Emily's father, Edward Dickinson, worked hard at restoring the family's name. As the oldest son, Edward Dickinson followed in his father's footsteps in many ways. He attended grammar school at the Amherst Academy, the school established by his father. He then went on to Yale University, in New Haven, Connecticut. He studied law. Like his father, Edward Dickinson became a leading lawyer of Amherst and one of its most prominent citizens. Edward Dickinson was involved in many of Amherst's civic projects. He was a founder of the Massachusetts Agricultural College and also helped to establish the local waterworks. He later worked hard to bring the railroad to Amherst—an important achievement because it connected the small town to the rest of the world and helped it thrive.

Edward Dickinson was also involved in politics. He was elected to the Massachusetts legislature in 1838 as a state representative, and served as a state senator from 1842 to 1844. In 1852, he served as a delegate to the National Whig Party Convention in Baltimore, Maryland. (The Whig party was an early political party. Many of its former members would go on to form the Republican party.) That same year, he was elected to U.S. Congress as a representative, an endeavor at which his father had failed years earlier. In 1854, he was admitted to argue cases before the U.S. Supreme Court, a point of distinction for lawyers to this day.

Young Emily once wrote that "Father is too busy with his Briefs [legal writing]—to notice what we do."[3] He was a renowned speaker who gave rousing speeches on holidays and special town occasions. At times it did seem as if Edward Dickinson was absorbed by his work, and he could be strict with his children. But he did have a creative side. He wrote poetry as a young man and loved to read. He had an extensive library and always encouraged his children to read and learn.

Edward Dickinson wrote essays for a magazine, the *New England Inquirer*. In one review of a poem by William Wordsworth (who became one of Emily's favorites), he wrote: "Along with the delicious melodies which he pours forth, he has thought on every page."[4]

Despite his absorption in his career, Edward Dickinson was a man of thought himself, spending time discussing literature, art, and philosophy. He believed that, in many ways, women should be considered equal to men. In a letter he wrote to his fiancée, Emily Norcross, in August 1826, Edward Dickinson described his meeting with a female author, Catharine Maria Sedgwick, who lived in New England. Sedgwick wrote books about American Indians. She depicted them as human beings with their own culture and families, and more than just "savages" to be conquered, as they were often portrayed at the time. Edward Dickinson wrote to his fiancée that Sedgwick was developing a distinctively American literature. As a result, he felt "a conscious pride that women of our own country & our own state, too, are emulating not only the females but the men of England & France & Germany & Italy in works of literature."[5]

This was a bold statement for a man to make in 1826, a time when women primarily were raised to be wives and mothers, not to have careers. It provides some insight into the ways he later might have

Two Women Writers in New England

In the early nineteenth century, Catharine Maria Sedgwick was one of the most famous authors in America. During her life, she wrote *A New-England Tale; or, Sketches of New-England Character and Manners* (1822), *Redwood* (1824), and many short stories and essays. Her most popular novel, *Hope Leslie* (1827), illustrated the cultural struggles between American Indians and the English colonists. She wrote it in response to James Fenimore Cooper's *Last of the Mohicans*. *Hope Leslie* portrayed American Indians in a positive light at a time when the colonists viewed American Indians as wild savages.

Lydia Maria Child, wrote *Hobomok: A Tale of Early Times* (1824). It was a story about a young colonial girl who marries an American Indian. The story was shocking in its day. Child wrote several other novels during her lifetime and became an abolitionist and political activist. In 1833, Child published the antislavery *An Appeal in Favor of that Class of Americans Called Africans*. She also served as editor of the *National Anti-Slavery Standard* from 1841 to 1843.

influenced his own daughter to be creative. At the very least, he did not frown on Emily's writing.

Emily's mother, Emily Norcross, was the third of nine children. She grew up on a farm just twenty miles south of Amherst in Monson, Massachusetts.

Emily Norcross attended boarding school in New Haven, Connecticut, at the same time that Edward Dickinson was at Yale. It was somewhat unusual to send a young woman to school so far from home, and the fact that her parents did so underscores their belief, just like the Dickinsons', that it was just as important to educate girls as it was to educate boys.

School for young women in the nineteenth century consisted of training that would help them become good mothers and wives. Their coursework usually consisted of reading, penmanship, embroidery, etiquette, sewing, and some kind of natural science like botany, the study of plants. Emily Norcross was not a particularly distinguished student at age nineteen, but she did earn at least one certificate of achievement, something that her daughter Emily kept for years as a treasured memento. It read: "Miss Emily Norcross, for punctual attendance, close application, good acquirements, and discreet behavior merits the approbation [approval] of her preceptress [teacher]."[6] In today's terms, the certificate meant that Emily's mother was a model student who came to class on time, paid attention, and did not talk out of turn.

Despite her "discreet behavior," outside of class Emily Norcross was described as a lively and witty young woman with a friendly disposition—traits she would pass on to her daughters. She was very sociable but struggled with homesickness. She wrote to her younger sister Lavinia Norcross that while she loved school, she longed for *"dear, dear* home."[7]

All of these qualities appealed to Edward Dickinson, who had a hard time living away from home himself. In a letter to Emily Norcross, Edward Dickinson wrote that while he felt he was "naturally quick & ardent [passionate] in my feelings," and "easily excited," Emily Norcross was "resolute—decided—rather particular."[8] He added that she was kind, and would put others' needs before her own. These were exactly the good qualities that he wanted a lady to possess, he said.

Being told that one of her best qualities is putting others' needs before her own might not sweep a young woman off her feet today, but Edward Dickinson did paint a picture of the ideal nineteenth-century woman. At that time many people believed that a woman should be modest, quiet, and sweet-tempered, but capable of running an efficient household. Running a household included cooking, baking, washing, ironing, cleaning, gardening, making soap, caring for children, and tending the livestock. Marriage was often more of a social contract than a romantic venture. When Edward Dickinson proposed to Emily Norcross, he advised her to take her time to decide. So she did. She thought about it for a full year before saying yes.

May Wedding

As she prepared for her wedding day in Monson, Massachusetts, Emily Norcross wrote her future husband that her friends were making farewell visits to her. Amherst was only twenty miles from Monson, not too far away to *ever* visit.

When a woman became a wife, however, her life changed dramatically. Marriage marked the shift from girlhood to womanhood. In addition, at the time, it was not uncommon for women to die in childbirth. Many women became pregnant shortly after their wedding day, only to die during labor less than a year later. Emily Norcross told Edward Dickinson, "I have many friends call upon me as they say to make their farewell visit. How do you suppose this sounds in my ear?" Her reluctance seems understandable. It is only when she adds, "But my dear it is to go and live with you," that there is an inkling that she is looking forward to becoming a wife.[9]

Edward Dickinson, too, showed signs of nervousness. He wrote to his wife-to-be, "The time is short, My Dear, and we shall probably soon have occasion to enter upon the serious duties of life—Are we prepared?"[10] Prepared or not, the two married in

Monson, Massachusetts, on May 6, 1828. The marriage brought together their equal love of home and family, admiration for nature, intellectual curiosity, and a desire for learning. It was this last quality that would influence the life of their oldest daughter, Emily Elizabeth Dickinson, and would help shape her into the poet she would become. Years later, the poet summed up her feelings of marriage when she wrote:

> *She rose to his requirement, dropped*
> *The playthings of her life*
> *To take the honorable work*
> *Of woman and of wife.*[11]

The Dickinson Children: Austin, Emily, and Lavinia

The newlyweds made their first home in Amherst, living with a widow named Jemima Montague. Edward Dickinson struggled to establish his career while his wife, Emily, kept house. Their family quickly grew, and they named their children after family members. Their son, William Austin (known as Austin), was born on April 16, 1829. A year later, Edward Dickinson purchased half of the Dickinson Homestead from his father and shared it with his parents and siblings for three years. Emily was born in that house on December 10, 1830. Emily's younger sister, Lavinia Norcross Dickinson (known by everyone as "Vinnie"), was born on February 28, 1833. That same year, Emily's grandfather, Samuel Fowler Dickinson, lost his fortune. The Dickinson home had to be sold. Emily's father, however, continued to rent the east half of the house, while another family lived in the west half.

It was a strange living arrangement, to be sure. Compounding that was an illness Emily's mother suffered after the birth of Lavinia in 1833. Little Emily was sent to stay for a month with her Aunt Lavinia Norcross in Monson. While there, Emily grew very attached to her aunt, and the Norcross family took good care of her. Throughout her life, Emily never forgot her Aunt Lavinia, who remained a constant favorite.

The Dickinson family had been sharing the Homestead with another family for several years. Edward Dickinson was anxious to provide for his family financially. He wrote to his wife from Boston in 1835 that he was bound and determined to make his fortune. As a result of his ambition, he was elected treasurer of Amherst College in 1835. In 1837, Edward Dickinson purchased land in the "West" in present-day Michigan in hopes of improving the family's situation. In 1840, the family—including eleven-year-old Austin, ten-year-old Emily, and seven-year-old Lavinia—moved to their own house on Pleasant Street just across from the school.

Young Emily and Austin felt it was a luxury to have a whole house to themselves.

Learning to Read and Write

Emily was five years old when she began attending primary school in a two-story brick building on Pleasant Street. Austin was already going to school there. They both learned to read and write there. While he was away in Boston, Edward wrote to Austin, Emily, and even little Lavinia, advising them to work hard at school.[12]

Years later, Emily wrote a poem about the joy of being let out of school on Saturday afternoon. Reading her words, one can easily imagine the students happily leaving school. Dickinson loved school, although in the poem she equates school with jail. She notes in the poem that it is ironic that even eager students like herself look forward to being let out of school to do as they please.

> From all the jails the boys and girls
>   Ecstatically [very happily] leap,—
> Beloved, only afternoon
>   That prison doesn't keep.
> They storm the earth and stun the air,
>   A mob of solid bliss.
> Alas! that frowns could lie in wait
>   For such a foe as this![13]

3

SCHOOL DAYS AND EARLY CORRESPONDENCE

Emily Dickinson, by all accounts, had a happy childhood. Although she sometimes felt that her parents did not understand her, they loved her dearly. She was extremely close to Austin and Vinnie. Together, the three of them had many friends, and there was always much activity going on at the Dickinson household. Emily Dickinson later wrote to a friend that there were "two things I have lost with Childhood—the rapture of losing my shoe in the Mud and going Home barefoot wading for Cardinal flowers and the mothers reproof which was more for my sake than her weary own, for she frowned with a smile."[1]

The comment reflects Dickinson's free-spirited childhood as well as insight into her relationship with her mother. Emily Norcross Dickinson was completely absorbed in the duties of being a wife and running the household. Practically speaking, this allowed little Emily the time to play and have fun— and later on, to write.

A Literary Mind

Emily Dickinson was bright, energetic, sentimental, and interested in life around her. By age fourteen, she had developed some political opinions and declared herself a Whig. She played the piano and was very interested in plants. Books and writing became important to Emily Dickinson very early on in her life. As a young girl, she had portraits of poets, novelists, and philosophers such as George Eliot, Elizabeth Barrett Browning, and Thomas Carlyle up in

Ralph Waldo Emerson was a transcendentalist philosopher and poet. Emerson influenced Emily Dickinson, who shared his love of nature and love of poetry.

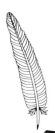

Jane Eyre

Charlotte Brontë's *Jane Eyre* is the story of a young woman who falls in love with Mr. Rochester, the father of the little girl for whom she is a nanny. Jane Eyre is a free-spirited young woman but a social outsider. The story illustrates the struggles Jane Eyre goes through, and her desire for spiritual and emotional fulfillment. Brontë was born in England in 1816. She wrote *Jane Eyre* in 1847. Her sisters, Emily and Anne, also wrote novels. Emily Brontë wrote *Wuthering Heights* and Anne wrote *Agnes Gray*.[2]

her room. She had books by George Eliot; Henry Wadsworth Longfellow; Alfred Lord Tennyson; Robert and Elizabeth Barrett Browning; Nathaniel Hawthorne; Ralph Waldo Emerson; George Sand; Charlotte, Emily, and Anne Brontë; and William Wordsworth. Emily was especially fond of Charlotte Brontë's *Jane Eyre*. She liked *Jane Eyre* because it was a sentimental story that was dark and romantic.

Circle of Five

Emily attended the Amherst Academy intermittently from 1840 to 1847. One of her instructors at the Amherst Academy, Daniel Taggart Fiske, described her as "very bright, but rather delicate and frail looking."[3] Fiske taught Emily in 1842 and 1843. She was, he said, "an excellent scholar: of exemplary deportment [behavior], faithful in all school duties: but somewhat shy and nervous."[4] Even then, Emily's essays were extraordinary and she received a lot of positive attention for her ability to write well.

Dickinson became part of a group of friends who called themselves the Circle of Five. The circle included Abiah Root, Sara Tracy, Harriet Merrill, Abby Maria Wood, and Emily. The girls wrote letters to one another, studied together, and had fun. Sometimes they argued, as friends do. "It is wonderful how the girls here do delight to bite & devour one another under the mask of friendship," Amherst Academy Principal Leonard Humphrey observed to a friend.[5]

Emily became especially close with Abiah Root. Abiah was one of Emily's earliest correspondents. Emily wrote to her until the girls were well into their twenties. Their friendship, however, dwindled as they grew older, after Abiah married and moved away.

Death of a Friend

In the spring of 1844, one of Emily's close friends, Sophia Holland, became sick. Emily stayed by her friend's bedside while Sophia's illness grew worse. When the doctor stopped allowing visitors, Emily explained that not being able to see her friend terrified her. After Emily was at last able to see Sophia one final time before she died, she described her friend as lying in bed "mild & beautiful as in health & her pale features lit up with an unearthly—smile."[6] Emily's description of her dying friend is a haunting one—Sophia is described in ghostly terms. She is pale and the only indication that she is still alive is her "unearthly—smile."

In April 1844, Sophia died. Emily became so upset over Sophia's death that her parents once again sent her to stay with her beloved Aunt Lavinia Norcross for a month in Boston. She wrote to Abiah Root that Sophia "was too lovely for earth & she was transplanted from earth to heaven."[7] Emily Dickinson viewed death as a mysterious and beautiful transition to eternity. One of her early poems about death captures her experience:

> *As by the dead we love to sit,*
> *Become so wondrous dear,*
> *As for the lost we grapple,*
> *Though all the rest are here,—*
>
> *In broken mathematics*
> *We estimate our prize,*
> *Vast, in its fading ratio,*
> *To our penurious [poor] eyes![8]*

Throughout her life, Emily Dickinson would maintain a correspondence with Sophia Holland's parents.

Last Days at Amherst Academy

In the spring of 1846, when she was sixteen, Emily Dickinson became ill. She had a very bad cold that she could not get rid of. As a result of her illness, she missed school. But when she recovered enough, Emily spent her time outside, roaming around the countryside.

Her parents sent her to Boston in mid-August 1846 to visit her Aunt Lavinia Norcross. Her aunt took her to many concerts and museums. She even toured the statehouse. During her month-long visit, she contemplated the depth of her religious feelings. To believe in God and be very religious was what everyone did at the time—it was a way to conform, or do what everyone else was doing. But Emily was a nonconformist. She could not bring herself to join the church, as the rest of the girls in her circle did. "I am still a stranger to the delightful emotions which fill your heart," she wrote to Abiah Root.[9] Emily was in love with the world and the beauty it had to offer. Religious teaching, she felt, would require her to reject the world.[10]

Emily returned to Amherst in September 1846, but she did not go back to the academy that fall. Instead, she stayed at home and helped her mother around the house. She also played the piano, sewed, and sent letters to her friends. She sent letters to

Austin, who was away at school. Emily went back to school the next semester.

Emily loved school, so she was anxious to return. But in January 1847, she caught the flu and was sick for nearly a month. She did not really start back at school until March, when she took classes in algebra, religious history, and the Classics—the study of Greek, Latin, and ancient civilizations.

She admired many of her teachers at the Amherst Academy, but she especially liked the principal, Leonard Humphrey, who taught Greek. When he died in 1850, Emily Dickinson wrote of her sadness in a letter to Abiah Root: "My master has gone to rest, and the open leaf of the book, and the scholar at school *alone*, make the tears come, and I cannot brush them away."[11]

Mount Holyoke

At sixteen, Emily went away to Mount Holyoke Seminary, a girls' school that was not far from Amherst. Because their parents strongly believed in the importance of education, all three Dickinson children were sent away to school. Vinnie was sent to Ipswich Female Seminary, and Austin was sent to Williston Seminary in Easthampton.

Mount Holyoke was directed by Mary Lyon, a woman whom Emily respected a great deal. Today, Mount Holyoke is a very prestigious college for women, largely due to Lyon's efforts. Emily studied for months to prepare for the entrance examinations. She said afterward that they were very tough, and many girls left because the exams were too difficult.[12]

Emily Dickinson roomed with her cousin Emily Norcross. The academics were rigorous. A typical day for Emily Dickinson began with breakfast at 7 A.M., followed by an hour of study hall at 8 A.M. Prayers were held between 9 and 10. History class began at 10:15, and English at 11. The girls had fifteen minutes of exercise at noon, and lunch was at

Pictured is commencement day at Mount Holyoke College. Dickinson attended Mount Holyoke but did not graduate.

12:30 P.M. At 1:30, Emily had 30 minutes of singing lessons. She practiced the piano for an hour, beginning at 2:45. At 3:45 they all met to talk about their day, and received praise or reprimand from Lyon if they were late for class, talked during quiet study hall, or had visitors in their room. "Unless we have a good & reasonable excuse for failure upon any of the items," Emily wrote to Abiah Root, "they are recorded & a *black mark* stands against our names."[13]

Dickinson was a bright student. She did very well because she was very creative. If she did not know the answer to a question, she would give such an imaginative answer that the teacher would pass her anyway.

Lyon was also very concerned with the girls' religious life. Emily had her doubts about organized religion, though Lyon tried very hard to convince each and every girl to focus on her spirituality. "This P.M. the names of the professors of religion, those who have a hope, and those who have not, were taken," Emily wrote. By "professors of religion," she meant those girls who believed in God. The girls who have hope were the ones who were *close* to declaring their faith. The ones without hope were the girls who did not believe in God. "I cannot tell you how solemn it was, as one after another class arose. I saw more than one weep as her name was put down '*no hope.*'"[14]

Emily struggled with her religious faith a great deal. On the one hand, she wanted to please Lyon. But on the other hand, she did not really believe in organized religion. She believed in God and avidly read the Bible. But her belief focused on how God made the world; how God made flowers bloom and bees buzz. Emily's parents did not share her belief that organized religion was not necessary. They were both strong Congregationalists and were very active in the church. Emily seemed to embrace another version of religious faith, one that was closer to transcendentalism, which was evolving not far from Amherst at the time. Transcendentalists believed that people could only learn about God through reason, which they defined as a person's own ability to figure out what is absolutely true.

Edward Hitchcock

Edward Hitchcock gave a lecture at Mount Holyoke during Emily's first semester in the fall of 1847. The theme of the lecture was Revelation, Emily's favorite book of the Bible. She referred to it as the "Gem chapter" because it describes heaven as made of precious stones like emeralds, sapphires, topazes, and amethysts.[15] The vivid imagery was something Emily enjoyed. Edward Hitchcock taught

Edward Hitchcock's lectures on nature combined scientific, religious, and poetic language.

botany, geology, and earth science at Amherst College. (Geology is the study of rocks and minerals, and earth science is the study of the earth and its development.) Hitchcock greatly improved Amherst college's science department. Initially, he was the professor of chemistry and natural history, but he changed that title to professor of theology—the study of religion—and geology. His approach to science appealed to Emily, who would later incorporate themes on religion and nature in her writing.

Before Hitchcock came to Amherst, he was a Congregational minister and a scholar who studied at Yale University. He was very religious and used his scientific research to increase and explain his faith in God. Emily attended his lectures and read some that were published. She was greatly affected by what she heard and read. Hitchcock had a lecture for each season. In his lecture "The Euthanasia of Autumn," Hitchcock provided a scientific explanation on the changing season by using the vivid language of a poet. Using imaginative language, Hitchcock explained how the leaves change color when the weather cools.[16] The resulting colors, he said, were:

> the richest and most diverse hues that nature can produce by the separation and blending of all the prismatic colors, meet us in every grove, and hill side, and mountain. Red of every shade, from crimson to cherry,—yellow, from bright sulphur to orange,— brown, from clove brown to liver brown,—and green, from grass green to oil green.[17]

Hitchcock's explanation that nature, with its cycles of the seasons, is the sublime creation of God, was a tremendous influence on Emily Dickinson and her writing.

Longing for Home

At Mount Holyoke, Emily was often homesick. "You may laugh at the idea, that I cannot be happy when away from home," she wrote to Abiah Root, explaining that the six weeks she had spent away from home were difficult. Emily was more than ready to go home at Thanksgiving in 1847. Although she traveled by carriage during a terrible storm, she said "never did Amherst look more lovely to me, and gratitude rose in my heart to God, for granting me such a safe return to my *own dear home.*"[18]

Emily spent her Thanksgiving playing games with friends and enjoying her family. Emily appeared

This famous portrait is of a young Emily Dickinson.

to be concerned with her looks and friends. "I am growing hand-some," she wrote in one letter, sounding half serious and half joking. "I expect I shall be the belle of Amherst when I reach my seventeenth year. I don't doubt but that I shall have perfect crowds of admirers at that age."[19] She described herself as having red hair, pale white skin, and a "long upper lip"[20] Other people described her as being of medium height and average weight with very white skin, chestnut hair, and brown eyes.[21]

Emily did not return to Mount Holyoke that winter because she caught a bad cold. She was tutored at home. Between 1847 and 1849, Benjamin Franklin Newton tutored Emily in literature. Newton was studying law under the direction of her father. The practice was known as "reading for the Bar." That meant that Newton would be a sort of legal apprentice until he knew enough to pass an exam called the Bar and be admitted to practice law and appear in court. Newton was very important to Emily as both a teacher and a friend. He helped shape Emily's religious views. He believed that the human soul was reflected in the harmony of nature. This view helped to ease Emily's struggle with organized religion and shift her spiritual focus to the sublime beauty found in the natural world.

Newton was probably the first person to recognize Emily's creative genius. He certainly was the first person who realized that Emily was a poet. He gave Emily Dickinson her first book of poems by Ralph Waldo Emerson when she was twenty years old. The poems, she said, "touched the secret Spring" of her heart and soul.[22] When Newton died of tuberculosis in 1853, Dickinson mourned his death in her writing, and called him "the first of my own friends."[23]

Traveling Preachers

No fewer than eight religious revivals came through Amherst between 1840 and 1862. A traveling minister would come to town, set up a large tent, and preach fiery sermons about the importance of believing in God. The aim was to save people's souls by converting them to Christianity. Everyone in town would attend, and several of Emily's friends were caught up in the religious frenzy. Emily, however, remained troubled. "Does not Eternity appear dreadful to you?" she wrote to Abiah Root in 1846.[24] Emily could not bring herself to formally join the Congregationalist Church and become a practicing Christian. Not belonging to a church was almost unheard of at the time. But Emily had a different way of looking at things—a "slant" as she called it— which did not follow an organized religion. Emily Dickinson found God in the world of nature. On one Sunday, Emily was adamant that she would *not* go to church. The more her father insisted, the more stubborn she became. Finally, when it was time to leave, no one could find her. Emily hid in the cellar, finding the darkness preferable to being forced to worship God in a constrained way that made her feel uncomfortable.

Austin and Vinnie

Austin went to Amherst College, and in 1850 he went to Harvard Law School. While at Harvard, Austin made friends with Joseph Lyman. Lyman visited the Dickinsons quite often during summers and holidays. Emily Dickinson had a crush on him— as did Vinnie—and both young women were quietly devastated when he married one of his southern cousins. After Austin graduated from Harvard, he stayed in Boston to teach, just to have the experience of being away from home.

Austin was very similar to his father. Both of them enjoyed beautiful horses. Austin wanted to go to a big city like Detroit or Chicago to practice law, but his father offered to build him a house next to the Dickinson Homestead. Edward Dickinson was becoming a very prestigious member of the community around this time. He was elected to the Massachusetts Senate, and he used his influence to make improvements in both Amherst College and the town.

The Dickinson household was usually the center of social activity. During graduation week at Amherst

Seniors march at Amherst College on graduation day. Since Edward Dickinson was connected to the college, commencement week was always full of parties for the Dickinson family.

College, the Dickinson family hosted a series of parties that all the faculty and graduates came to with their families. When his father suggested he stay and live in Amherst, Austin stayed in Amherst.

As the sisters grew older, Vinnie assumed the role of family caretaker. Even though Vinnie was younger, she was more decisive and assertive. "Vinnie demurs, Vinnie decides," Dickinson once said of her protective sister.[25] The two sisters were very close. Vinnie, Dickinson wrote, "has no father and mother but me, and I no parents but her."[26] Their parents were certainly present in the home, but the sisters protected one another in various ways. As Vinnie became more sociable with many friends and admirers, Dickinson moved more into the background. When Vinnie was eighteen, Dickinson wrote to Austin at Harvard that their younger sister was growing *"perter* [more lively] and more pert day by day."[27] Like her older siblings, Vinnie was extremely witty and funny, and she would entertain her friends by impersonating people. Vinnie's roommate at Ipswich Female Seminary, Jane Hitchcock, said that without Vinnie, life at school would have been unbearable.

Around 1847, Emily met Susan Gilbert. The two young women met either through mutual friends at the Amherst Academy or the sociable Vinnie. They were the same age, but Sue Gilbert was in many ways Emily's opposite. Sue was orphaned at a young age and was extremely outgoing and sociable. Dickinson was more shy. Sue loved to travel. Emily always wanted to be back home. But both young women were smart and witty, and they forged a complex friendship that lasted their entire lives.

One of Emily Dickinson's first letters to Sue was written in December 1850.[28] Dickinson is writing to comfort Sue, whose sister had just died. "Remember lonely one—tho, <u>she</u> comes not to us, <u>we</u> shall return to <u>her</u>!"[29] In the numerous letters the two women exchanged over the years, Dickinson refers to Sue as "Vesuvius" and "Sister Sue." Some of Dickinson's poems were written directly to or for Sue Gilbert. Often, Dickinson would write a draft of a poem or a letter and give it to Sue to critique. It was the way the two friends communicated, and it reflected the special bond they shared.

4

THE WRITING LIFE

The next ten years of Dickinson's life were filled with creativity. She wrote nearly a thousand poems, most of them enclosed in letters to Sue Gilbert and other friends. One of the first poems she sent to Gilbert is about two of Dickinson's central themes: writing and eternity. Dickinson calls upon Gilbert (as the reader) to use writing to navigate through the storms of life to the "silent west." In this case, "west" symbolizes eternity—peaceful rest:

> On this wondrous sea
>   Sailing silently,
> Knowest thou the shore
>   Ho! pilot, ho!

Where no breakers roar,
Where the storm is o'er?

In the silent west
Many sails at rest,
Their anchors fast;
Thither I pilot thee,—
Land, ho! Eternity!
Ashore at last![1]

This is Dickinson's way of telling her friend to write to her. Writing was central to their friendship. Gilbert's letters sustained Dickinson and helped her get through her day. Dickinson, in turn, wrote many letters to Gilbert. She told Gilbert everything. In the poem, Dickinson seems to say that she will comfort Gilbert. Dickinson tells Gilbert that *she* will navigate Gilbert through the stormy waters, safely to a heavenly shore. That is how important Sue Gilbert was to Emily Dickinson.

Growing Older

Vinnie turned eighteen years old in February 1851. She wrote in her diary that she celebrated the day by going to a lecture and shopping with a friend. She had friends over to her house that evening. "I am 18 years old today, rather old girl," she wrote in her diary.[2] The two sisters discussed growing older one day as they sat sewing. When Vinnie said she thought twenty was getting old, Dickinson said she did not care about growing older at all. She was rather looking forward to it, she said.

On Dickinson's twenty-first birthday later that year, Dickinson had Abiah Root and Abby Palmer over for supper. She did contemplate getting older—although it came out in a lighthearted way. She wrote to Sue Gilbert that, as an old woman, "it would be a comfort to have a piping voice, and a broken back, and scare little children."[3]

Going to Boston

Dickinson and Vinnie went to see Austin in the fall of 1851. The sisters traveled by train, first to Worcester, then on to Boston. They visited with their Aunt Lavinia Norcross and other family friends, toured Austin's school, and went to museums and concerts. The high point of the visit, though, was going to an ice cream parlor. The sisters went several times during their three-week visit.

Once the sisters returned home, Dickinson wrote to Austin that Amherst was very lonely without him.[4] Despite her attachment to home and family, she would rather be with Austin, Dickinson said. This sentiment points to how close the Dickinson siblings were. For his part, Austin described his sisters' visit in a letter to Sue Gilbert, with whom he had become acquainted. His description of their visit perfectly illustrates how he viewed his sisters' opposite temperaments. "Vinnie enjoyed herself, as she always does among strangers—Emily became confirmed in her opinion of the hollowness & awfulness of the *world*."[5] Vinnie loved being around people and was lively, while Dickinson was more critical of society and its conventions. She was more comfortable with the natural world.

In 1851, Gilbert left Amherst unexpectedly to teach at a girls' school in Baltimore, Maryland. Everyone thought she was crazy to leave Amherst for a busy city like Baltimore. It was so dangerous there compared to the quiet streets of Amherst. But Gilbert loved living in a large city—and it was a matter of independence for her to leave the relative safety of Amherst and to live on her own. She made many friends and everyone thought she was very entertaining and funny when she would impersonate the schoolmaster.

Emily Dickinson missed Gilbert terribly during the year she was in Baltimore. Sue was her closest friend. Dickinson wrote long, imaginative letters to Gilbert. She told Gilbert what she was doing, who she was visiting, and which books she was reading. In her letters to Gilbert, Dickinson often told her how she could not wait until the year was up and Gilbert would come home to Amherst. "I sit here with my little whip, cracking the time away, till not an hour is left of it—then you are here!"[6] she wrote.

Although Dickinson did tell Gilbert to have "all the fun wh[ich] you possibly can, and laugh as often and sing, for tears are plentier than smiles in this little world of ours."[7]

While Gilbert loved living on her own, Austin did not like being away from Amherst. He wrote to Sue that he felt disconnected from all of the hustle and bustle of the city. It was not the place for him. When he decided to return home to Amherst, Dickinson rejoiced. "Duty is black and brown— home is bright and shining," she told him.[8] Anticipating his arrival, she sent him a poem about the perfection of home.

Home was a safe haven, but Dickinson was not always content. Dickinson often seemed to get the winter blues. On April 30, 1851, she wrote, "sewed and ironed all day, Mother is sick. Raining merrily. Feel Blue! Blue!"[9]

Dickinson found housekeeping wearisome work that consumed time she would rather spend writing letters and poems. Over the years, she let Vinnie take charge of the cleaning and cooking. But Dickinson always baked the bread because her father liked it best. She also baked cakes and treats for friends.

On a typical day, Dickinson and her sister would sew, read, clean, and cook. The young women had private tutors come to give them lessons in subjects like literature and ancient history. Sometimes friends came over, and the group of young people would play games in the house or enjoy some recreation outside. In early spring, Emily Dickinson and her friends tapped the maple trees. They collected the sap in buckets and then made maple syrup with it.

Dickinson's moods sometimes caused her to clash with her father. Usually, when Austin and Vinnie were home, they created enough space between Dickinson and her father. But now, Austin's absence drained Dickinson. She often felt sad, and she told her brother that she was just as likely to cry as to laugh at anything funny. She missed the good times they had when Austin was at home. "We don't have many jokes tho' *now*, it is pretty much all sobriety [seriousness]," Dickinson wrote to Austin. Describing what it was like without him, Dickinson hints that home was not always peaceful. "And we do not have much poetry, father having made up his mind that its pretty much all *real life*. Father's real life and *mine* sometimes come in collision, but as yet, escape unhurt!"[10]

Today, many people think that Dickinson's moodiness was really a form of depression. It is understandable, though, that being cooped up during the long New England winters would make her feel miserable and restless. Whatever the cause, her moods affected her creativity. Sometimes, when she was in a certain mood, she would stay up all night and write.

While Austin was teaching in Boston, Dickinson kept him abreast of what was happening at home. The Dickinson family went to hear Jennie Lind sing. Jennie Lind was a young Swedish girl whose singing was very popular in the mid-1800s. Her voice was so distinctive that she was nicknamed the "Swedish Nightingale." After the family went to hear Jennie Lind, Dickinson told Austin that she thought the singer was lovely, but that their usually serious father spent the evening looking uncharacteristically *"mad* and *silly,* and yet so much amused that you would have *died* laughing."[11]

"The Slightest in the House"

As she spent more time writing, Emily Dickinson began to withdraw from society. "I was the slightest in the House," she once said of herself.[12] Perhaps she was smallest in size, but her comment implies that she was "small" because she kept to herself. Dickinson began writing poetry when she was a teenager, and by the mid-1850s was writing even more intensely. She copied and bound her poems into fascicles. Her writing desk faced Main Street so she could observe everyone's coming and goings—it was a way for her to keep in touch with people without ever having to leave her room.

Even as she baked bread and cakes for the family, she would keep paper and a pencil nearby. She would write down her thoughts as she looked out the kitchen window into the garden. Dickinson also grew exotic plants and flowers, cultivating seedlings brought to her by friends. She grew jasmine in a greenhouse her father built especially for her, and tended to a half-acre garden.

Dickinson read the poems of Samuel Taylor Coleridge and the other British Romantic poets such as William Blake and William Wordsworth. She also

Emily Dickinson's garden can still be visited today. Above is a view of the garden from the Homestead.

read the King James Bible, Emily Brontë's *Jane Eyre*, and the works of Shakespeare. These books and authors influenced her own writing—Shakespeare and the King James Bible probably most of all. She often incorporated references to certain plays or passages in her poetry.

Many of her poems were about death, nature, and eternity. Victorian culture encouraged this kind of contemplation, but to today's readers, Dickinson's thoughts seem excessive. Years later she was described as being preoccupied with death, and solemn, but not sad.[13]

Dickinson was not the only poet in the family. Her Aunt Elizabeth Dickinson—one of her father's younger sisters—wrote a family history in verse for the August 1883 family reunion. It was fifty-seven quatrains (a group of four lines of poetry) long, and newspapers in Boston and Worcester reprinted the poem.

Austin also tried his hand at verse. Dickinson teased him about his literary attempts in a letter dated March 27, 1853. Despite her teasing, she admits that she has been writing poems also, and that he just might be crossing over into her territory. "I've been in the habit *myself* of writing some few things," she said, "so you'd better be somewhat careful, or I'll call the police!"[14]

Sister Sue

By 1854, Emily Dickinson was sending Sue Gilbert her poetry. Gilbert understood Dickinson's poetry and her outlook on the world. The entire Dickinson family adored Gilbert's lively manner and quick wit. Dickinson encouraged Austin's interest in her friend as a way to keep Sue in the family.

Austin sent Sue Gilbert passionate love letters while he was in Boston. "I love you Sue up to the very highest strain my nature can bear," he wrote in 1853.[15] Austin and Gilbert had a tumultuous courtship. After they were engaged, their letters indicate that each considered breaking off the engagement at different times. Dickinson quietly seemed to be nudging Austin and Gilbert together. "I see more of Susie than of any other girl," Dickinson wrote Austin. "She said the last time I saw her, she hadn't had a 'talk since Austin went away.'"[16] Clearly, Dickinson was letting Austin know that Sue Gilbert found him more interesting to talk to than any other young man she knew.

Dickinson's efforts seemed to work. After a three-year engagement, Austin and Sue Gilbert married on July 1, 1856, in Geneva, New York. At the time, weddings were not the big events they are today. The ceremony was simple. None of the Dickinson family attended the wedding. Despite their absence, the Dickinson family most certainly

Austin and Sue spent their honeymoon in Niagara Falls. The location was a source of inspiration for many artists, including Frederick Church, of the Hudson River School.

approved of Sue Gilbert. For her part, Sue did not seem excited about her own wedding. In a letter to a family friend, Sue wrote: "I shall have a quiet wedding—a very few friends and my brothers & sisters a little cake—a little ice cream and it is all over—the millionth wedding since the world began."[17] Sue's attitude toward her wedding was surprisingly lacking in excitement.

For a time, it looked as if the couple would move west and settle in Chicago or Detroit, just as Austin wanted. Sue found this prospect exciting. However, Edward Dickinson offered to build a house for the newlyweds right next door to the Dickinson mansion. Austin agreed, and also went to work as a lawyer with his father.

Austin and Sue's home, known as the Evergreens, became the social center of Amherst. Sue loved to give parties, and Emily Dickinson attended them. She would play the piano, sing, or listen and talk with the many guests. When Ralph Waldo Emerson came to Amherst in 1857, he stayed with Sue and Austin. At this time, Dickinson seemed to enjoy having a vibrant social life. One visitor painted a vivid picture of the party atmosphere, calling it "celestial," with the "blazing *wood* fire—*Emily*—*Austin*—the music—the rampant fun—the inextinguishable laughter."[18] Dickinson loved having

Sue so close by. She said she had two sisters now, one in her house, "and one, a hedge away."[19]

Austin and Sue had three children. Edward Dickinson, known as Ned, was born in 1861, Martha Dickinson was born in 1866, and Thomas Gilbert Dickinson was born in 1875. But Sue and Austin ultimately had an unhappy marriage. Austin did not appreciate the constant parties thrown by the sociable Sue. He was quiet and introspective, or caught up in his own thoughts. As Austin and Sue's family grew, they took in two cousins, Clara and Anna Newman, to help. Beginning in 1858, the

The Evergreens (rear view pictured) was built for Austin and Sue by Edward Dickinson. It was his way of keeping his son close to home.

Newman sisters spent ten years living and working for the family.

Heading the "Committee on Arrangements"

As the years progressed, the vivacious Vinnie emerged as the practical one, cleaning and doing errands for the family. She even referred to herself as "head of the committee on arrangements."[20] Vinnie ran the household, and this allowed Dickinson the time to write.

Sometimes Dickinson appeared to lose patience with her orderly sister and mother when their zest for cleaning interfered with her creativity. When Vinnie and their mother gave the house a thorough cleaning, Dickinson wrote to Austin to complain. "We cleaned house [all last week]," Dickinson told him. "[That is to say]—Mother and Vinnie did—and I scolded because they moved my things. I can't find much [left anywhere], that I used to wear [or know of]. You will conceive that I am surrounded by trial."[21]

Despite sometimes being annoyed with her, Dickinson loved Vinnie. The two sisters were dependent on each other. When Vinnie spent a month in Boston with their Aunt Lavinia Norcross, Dickinson anxiously awaited her return. "I would like more sisters, that the taking out of one might not leave such stillness," she wrote. Her younger sister's absence made Dickinson realize how much she relied on Vinnie. "Vinnie has been all, so long, I feel the oddest fright at parting with her for an hour, lest a storm arise, and I go unsheltered."[22]

A Stony Heart?

By age twenty-four, it was becoming clear that Dickinson would not marry. She was carving out a niche for herself as a strong-minded individual—just as she had earlier in her refusal to embrace religion. She wrote to Sue that she must have a "hard heart of stone" because her heart just would not break over the "gallant men."[23]

While she was young, Dickinson never seemed to have found a man who fully understood her perspective on life. She wrote in a letter to Sue, "All men say 'What' to me."[24] Most men did not understand her use of metaphor or her constant references to nature.

Both Dickinson sisters had admirers and kept track of who came to visit them and how they spent their time. Mostly, when young men came to visit, they went on walks or were escorted to lectures, shopped, rode horseback, played games at home in the parlor, or played the piano and sang.

Dickinson did have many friends and people who cared about her. "*Emilie . . . sends me beautiful letters & each one makes me love her more,*" Eliza

Coleman wrote to a mutual acquaintance. "I know you appreciate her & I think few of her Amherst friends do. They wholly misinterpret her, I believe."[25]

Growing Prominence

Edward Dickinson was a very important and well-respected person in Amherst. He was influential in bringing the railroad to the country town. Dickinson broke the news to Austin, saying teasingly, "Father . . . went marching around the town . . . like some old Roman General, upon a Triumph Day."[26] It was a monumental event because it meant that Amherst would grow as a town and not be cut off from the rest of the world. Dickinson, in her usual exaggerated style, called it the "most *miraculous* event in the lives of us all."[27]

Edward Dickinson was elected to Congress in 1852. He represented Massachusetts's 10th Congressional District. He also was elected to be a delegate to the National Whig Convention in Baltimore. In the summer of 1852, Edward Dickinson traveled to Baltimore, where he nominated Daniel Webster for president. But Webster did not win the nomination. Winfield Scott did.

Austin, Vinnie, and their mother went to visit Edward Dickinson in Washington, D.C., in early 1854. Dickinson did not accompany them to the capital. Sue stayed to keep Dickinson company, as

The Whig Party

The nation's political parties were transformed during Emily Dickinson's life. The Whig party was formed around 1834 in opposition to the Democratic party and then-President Andrew Jackson. The Whigs were so named because during the American Revolution, people who opposed the king called themselves whigs. The Whig party believed that President Jackson, a Democrat from Tennessee, was assuming too much political power and not listening to Congress. Cartoonists of the day made fun of him, drawing him as King Andrew. The Whigs, led by senators Daniel Webster of Massachusetts and Henry Clay of Kentucky, declared themselves the defenders of individual liberties. The party focused on improving the nation's roads, banks, canals, and other internal national structures. Presidents William Henry Harrison, Zachary Taylor, and Millard Fillmore were members of the Whig party. However, after the deaths of Clay and Webster, the Whig party's popularity waned, and the party disintegrated in 1856.[28]

did a cousin, John Long Graves. Graves said years later that Dickinson would stay up late at night and play the piano. Recalling the time they spent together, Dickinson told him, "I play the old—odd tunes yet, which used to flit about your head after honest hours—and wake dear Sue, and madden me, with their grief and fun."[29]

The family went to Washington again in 1855. This time, Dickinson went too. They stayed in the famous Willard Hotel, which still operates today. Dickinson did not really like Washington. She thought it was full of pompous politicians. She did not enjoy the social aspect of it. Vinnie, on the other hand, loved the capital city. In particular, Vinnie enjoyed all of the parties and festivities associated with Congress. She was quite the social butterfly and developed a crush or two on some of her father's colleagues.[30]

Meeting the Mysterious Wadsworth

After spending two weeks at the Willard, the girls went to visit their cousin, Eliza Coleman, in Philadelphia. While in Philadelphia, it is believed that Dickinson went to hear the Reverend Charles Wadsworth preach at the Arch Street Presbyterian Church.[31] Wadsworth was an impressive speaker. Curiously, he was also something of a recluse; he rarely met with parishioners and other ministers. He wanted to be known for his sermons. Wadsworth made a distinct impression on Dickinson. He seemed very powerful and mysterious to her.

Over the years Dickinson and Wadsworth occasionally exchanged letters. There is some speculation that Wadsworth was the mysterious "Master" to whom Dickinson addressed some of her letters about writing. However, Wadsworth was a man who not only was a minister of the organized religion Dickinson avoided, but he felt that poetry was of little importance. Wadsworth at one time wrote poetry himself. But he ultimately rejected this type of writing for religion. He even wrote a sermon, "Religious Glorying," that rejected poetry as a relic of the past. Dickinson might have seen this sermon in particular. She received copies of Wadsworth's sermons from friends. So it is unlikely that Wadsworth was "Master."

Writing Very Fine Things

Emily Dickinson's Valentine's Day poem to a friend, William Howland, was published in the *Springfield Republican* in 1854. The paper's editor, Samuel Bowles, introduced her poem by saying that he hoped Dickinson would submit more for publication.

Dickinson sought to impress Sue with her writing, and would sometimes draft letters three times before sending them. Dickinson sought Sue's opinion on her writing. Dickinson sent the poem "Safe in the Alabaster Chambers" to Sue, asking if it was just right. The poem is about the dead waiting in their coffins for the resurrection while the rest of the world goes on without them. Sue wrote back that she did not think the second verse went with the first one. So Dickinson changed it to this:

Safe in their alabaster chambers,
Untouched by morning and untouched by noon,
Sleep the meek members of the resurrection,
Rafter of satin, and roof of stone.

Light laughs the breeze in her castle of sunshine;
Babbles the bee in a stolid ear;
Pipe the sweet birds in ignorant cadence,—
Ah, what sagacity [wisdom] perished here!

Grand go the years in the crescent above them;
Worlds scoop their arcs, and firmaments row,
Diadems [tiaras] drop and Doges surrender,
Soundless as dots on a disk of snow.[32]

Dickinson often sought feedback on her poems. Three letters to "Master" were found among her papers after her death. The letters appeared to be artistic efforts in their own right, as there were several drafts of them, indicating she would send them when she felt they were just right. The first letter was written in 1858. The second was written in the early 1860s, and the third was written shortly thereafter. But "Master's" identity remains unclear, even today.

5

STRANGE
TO SOME

In her writing, Dickinson deliberately skirted the obvious, taking a step away from the truth in order to maintain her privacy. As a result, her poetry is full of metaphors and symbols. She and Austin used to say that the truth should be told "slant." Through precise language, she sought to reveal the secret inner nature of the thing observed, but she revealed it indirectly. To her, it was gentler to reveal the truth in this way.

"Slant" is also how Dickinson approached publishing. She rarely sought publication directly. She sought it indirectly, sharing her poems and carefully crafted letters with friends. Emily Dickinson's poetry sometimes appeared in print, but only because someone else sent it to a publisher.

Death at Home

However, Dickinson's life continued to be marred by the loss of loved ones. Her Aunt Lavinia Norcross died in April 1860. "I sob and cry til I can hardly see around the house," Dickinson wrote to her sister, Vinnie, who had been staying with the Norcross family in Boston. Dickinson was devastated by her aunt's death and keenly felt her loss. Even in her grief, Dickinson's words of comfort to Vinnie are imaginative and stirring. "It is dark and strange to think of summer afterward! How she loved the summer! The birds keep singing just the same. Oh! The thoughtless birds!"[1]

Inspirations

The year 1862 marked the height of Dickinson's creativity. In that year alone she wrote nearly 366 poems. Many of her poems reflect the trope—using a word as a figure of speech—of love, loss, and Eternity.[2] By this time in her life, she had developed her own ideas about spirituality. She was able to convey her own concept of finding religion in nature. Some poems depict her as one with God, while other times she is a tiny speck in the universe. She wrote poems to friends and included them in her letters. Samuel Bowles, Sue Dickinson, the Hollands, Helen Hunt Jackson, her nephews and nieces, as well as cousins, friends, and neighbors received poems written to and for them. She was not secretly writing poetry. She was sharing it openly. Most likely she wrote in the early morning hours before sunrise. For Dickinson, morning symbolized renewal, inspiration, and immortality. Many of her poems incorporate references to light and the sunrise. These types of poems, written to honor the sunrise, are called aubades.

Dickinson's ideas for poems came from things found in nature, things she read, contemporary society, and even famous painters such as Thomas Cole and Frederick Church. Both painters were prominent members of the Hudson River school, a group of nineteenth-century artists who portrayed the sublime and magnificent in nature. In his paintings,

Hudson River School painter Thomas Cole was famous for his American landscapes. Two of his most popular series of paintings were "The Course of Empire" (1836) and "The Voyage of Life" (1840).

Thomas Cole commented on the relationship of the artist to nature and eternity.

Cole's work made a strong impression on Dickinson, particularly the "The Voyage of Life" painting series. These paintings were an allegory drawn from John Bunyan's novel *Pilgrim's Progress.* The novel was about one man's spiritual journey from Earth (and all its trials and temptation) to heaven. Dickinson used images similar to Cole's, such as the boat, the guardian angel, the masculine

Thomas Cole's Old Age *was part of a series of paintings on the journey through life called "The Voyage of Life." Dickinson was familiar with Cole's paintings and shared Cole's philosophy of life, nature, and art.*

figure of a youth embarking on a dramatic journey, and rough storms.

Dickinson also was familiar with Frederick Church's paintings. At the time she was writing, the artist was very popular. The unveiling of his paintings was a national event. His painting of Niagara Falls, completed in 1853, conveys the majestic power of the great waterfall. The painting is meant to evoke a feeling of serenity. It reflects the interplay between the rays of light and the dark, rushing water. Dickinson tried to capture this in her poetry about the landscape and eternity.

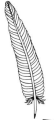

Hudson River School

The Hudson River School was the first American school of landscape painting. It was active from 1825 to 1870, a time when American artists were establishing their own style. Thomas Cole was an early leader. Other artists included Frederick Church, Asher Durand, John Kensett, Thomas Doughty, Jasper Cropsey, and John Casilear. The artists traveled through New York's Hudson Valley and the New England area searching for distinctively American images in the landscape. Many of their paintings depict the untamed American wilderness. The group is also referred to as Romantic Realists, as they combined detailed landscape images with themes and messages taken from contemporary literature.[3]

Finding Master?

Dickinson wrote to Thomas Wentworth Higginson in 1862, after reading an essay he wrote in a magazine, *The Atlantic Monthly*. Higginson was very liberal-minded. Like Ralph Waldo Emerson, he was educated at Harvard Divinity School and became a Unitarian minister. He supported women's rights and strongly opposed slavery. He was such an ardent abolitionist that he helped John Brown plan the 1859 raid on Harper's Ferry, Virginia (now in West Virginia), that helped spark the American Civil War.

Some say Higginson was the mysterious "Master" to whom Dickinson addressed several poems. If that is the case, Higginson was not a good mentor, because he did not understand Dickinson's unconventional poetry. He did not encourage her to publish. Dickinson first wrote to him on April 16, 1862, to comment on an essay he wrote, "Letter to a Young Contributor," that she had read in the magazine the *Atlantic Monthly*. What Thomas Higginson wrote in the essay, which was about an editor rejecting the work of a young writer, touched Dickinson. He wrote about nature and immortality—and the mysteries of the universe.

Inspired, Dickinson asked him to critique her poems. "Are you too deeply occupied to say if my Verse is alive?" she asked him. "Should you think it breathed—and had you the leisure to tell me, I should feel quick gratitude."[4] Dickinson asked if he would critique her poems without telling anyone. She sent him four poems: "Safe in their Alabaster Chambers," "The Nearest Dream recedes unrealized," "We Play at Paste," and "I'll tell you how the sun rose." The poems represented her major subjects—love, death, art, eternity, and the landscape—and how those themes related to nature.

Higginson responded immediately, and his letter was full of questions. Who was she and what did she read? How old was she? Where did she go to school? He was impressed by her poems and wanted to know more about her. When she first wrote to him, she enclosed her calling card. That was a card that had her name on it, sort of like a business card. By enclosing her card, she was letting him know that she was a woman from a respected family. After reading her poems, Higginson definitely wanted to know more.

In an April 25, 1862, letter to Higginson, Dickinson refers to his critique of her poems as "surgery," and thanked him because "it was not so painful as I supposed."[5] In her own indirect style, she described her life. "You ask me of my Companions Hills—Sir—and the Sundown—and a Dog—large as myself."[6] In that letter she included three more poems: "There came a Day at Summer's

Thomas Wentworth Higginson was Emily Dickinson's mentor and friend. He worked to get her poetry published after her death.

full," "Of all the Sounds dispatched abroad," and "South Winds jostle them." In another letter she described her physical appearance. She used similes—literary comparisons that use "like" or "as"—even to describe herself. She said she was small "like the Wren, and my Hair is bold, like the Chestnut Bur—and my eyes, like the Sherry in the Glass, that the Guest leaves."[7]

In her third letter to Higginson, dated June 7, 1862, Dickinson asked him to be her mentor, although she sounds a bit wary of his criticism. Dickinson may have been looking for someone to publish her poems. But Higginson discouraged her. "I smile when you suggest that I delay 'to publish,'" she wrote, noting that he thinks her writing style is "'spasmodic [irregular]'" and "'uncontrolled.'"[8] In many ways, he was her mentor. He was an expert in the field of publishing, and Dickinson may have believed that he had a lot to teach her. She continued to send him poetry, and he continued to critique it even though he never encouraged her to publish.

Selecting Her Own Society

All of the Dickinsons, beginning with Samuel Fowler Dickinson, were nervous and high strung. None of them particularly liked to travel. Emily Dickinson continued to gradually withdraw from society. However, she remained in touch with the world through her letters to and from her many friends and acquaintances. She kept abreast of the news and politics, reading the *Springfield Republican* as well as other publications every day.

Austin thought her decision not to greet callers was "painfully hollow."[9] What he meant was that Dickinson was just *trying* to be strange. But Vinnie said later that her older sister's strange behavior was not something Dickinson planned to do. She explained that it "was only a happen."[10] Dickinson was not trying to make a statement; she just quietly stopped greeting those who called on her. When neighbors or other nosy people would ask her why she did not make her older sister leave the house or greet guests, Vinnie would answer that her sister was perfectly happy and could do as she pleased.

Over the years, people speculated as to why Dickinson behaved so strangely. Some said that she had a quarrel with her father over a potential boyfriend. However, Vinnie tried to dispel that rumor, as she did with all gossip about the family. "We didn't know what it was, we in Amherst," said one woman who made dresses for Vinnie and Dickinson. "Everyone wondered. Everyone talked."[11]

Emily Dickinson's decision to remove herself from society appears to have been hers alone. Once, when her niece, Martha, was punished by being sent to her room, Dickinson sent a note to her saying, "Matty, child, no one could punish a Dickinson by shutting her up alone."[12] Solitude meant she was free to write, read, and think about what she wanted to. It was her freedom. It was her choice. Dickinson even wrote a poem about being particular about the people she saw and how she spent her time:

> *The soul selects her own society,*
> *Then shuts the door;*
> *On her divine majority*
> *Obtrude no more.*
> *Unmoved, she notes the chariot's pausing*
> *At her low gate;*

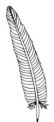

Transcendentalism

Henry David Thoreau and Ralph Waldo Emerson were part of a group of New England intellectuals who adhered to the philosophy of transcendentalism. The transcendentalist movement flourished between 1836 and 1860. Emerson even wrote an essay titled "Transcendentalism." The transcendentalists believed that God could be found in man and nature. They emphasized the strength of the individual and rejected the church's traditional authority. Thoreau even went so far as to reject governmental authority. The transcendentalists met in Boston and Concord to discuss philosophy, literature, and religion. The group included Margaret Fuller and Bronson Alcott.

Unmoved, an emperor is kneeling
Upon her mat.
I've known her from an ample nation
Choose one;
Then close the valves of her attention
Like stone.[13]

It was widely believed at the time that to be a true artist, one needed solitude. Henry David Thoreau wrote in *Walden* that he went to the woods "because I wanted to live deliberately."[14] Thoreau wanted to be unburdened by the pressures of everyday life in society. Dickinson followed the philosopher Ralph Waldo Emerson's advice to poets—that they should "build their own world."[15] Dickinson tried to do this. She constructed a world that marveled in the sunrise and springtime, and emphasized family and the great power of the imagination.

But Dickinson might have taken this to the extreme. By the mid-1860s she would

Like Emily Dickinson, Henry David Thoreau valued solitude when he needed to write or think about something. However, Dickinson withdrew from society more than Thoreau did.

literally run and hide when visitors arrived to see her. She often wore white, a Victorian tradition to indicate purity. She would lower cakes and cookies out of her bedroom window to the neighborhood children below. Her good friend Mabel Loomis Todd said that she withdrew because she was "disgusted with society."[16] Samuel Bowles, the editor of the *Springfield Republican*, called her the "Queen Recluse."[17]

Although she might have been withdrawing from society, she did not remove herself from the natural world. Around 1864, "The Snake" was published in the *Springfield Republican*. The poem vividly describes how the poet communes with nature—even a wily snake that startles her whenever she crosses his path:

> *Several of nature's people*
> *I know, and they know me;*
> *I feel for them a transport*
> *Of cordiality;*
>
> *But never met this fellow,*
> *Attended or alone,*
> *Without a tighter breathing,*
> *And zero at the bone.*[18]

The American Civil War

Unlike many women her age—such as Louisa May Alcott—Dickinson did not participate in the American Civil War effort. (In 1861, the Civil War had erupted between the North and the South over slavery and other issues.) She even refrained from being a nurse, which is what many women did in order to aid in the war effort. While Alcott and many other women did all they could to go to the battlefront as nurses, Dickinson stayed in Amherst. Her letters to friends and family during the war mourn the deaths of Amherst's soldiers. "Poor little widow's boy, riding to-night in the mad wind, back to the village burying ground where he never dreamed of sleeping," Dickinson described the death of one soldier and his soul's midnight journey back to the Amherst cemetery. She described death as "the dreamless sleep!"[19]

The Dickinson family opposed slavery. Dickinson's father said in 1855 that Americans should not let slavery spread to the rest of the country—a key issue in the country as people continued to move westward into territories like Missouri, Kansas, and Texas. A sometimes violent debate raged as to whether those territories should permit slavery. The Dickinson family did not believe that slavery should be permitted.

However, when Austin was drafted into the U.S. Army in the early 1860s, he paid another man to fight in his place. That man was known as a substitute. This was a common practice at the time for many wealthy Northern men. Austin never knew what happened to the man during the war. However, Austin was devastated when he learned that one of his good friends, Frazer Stearns, was killed at the Battle of New Bern in North Carolina in 1862. Stearns was the son of the president of Amherst College. Although Stearns could have paid someone to fight for him, he joined the Union Army, while Austin stayed behind. Austin's grief at his friend's death may have been tinged with guilt.

The Civil War must have seemed far away from Amherst. Most of the major battles took place in

Austin Dickinson's friend Frazer Stearns was killed at the Battle of New Bern. After New Bern was captured, it remained in the hands of the Union Army until the end of the war.

Virginia, Maryland, Pennsylvania, and the Carolinas. So Stearns's death brought the reality of war home to Amherst. Dickinson wrote to Samuel Bowles, explaining, "Austin is chilled—by Frazer's murder— He says—his Brain keeps saying over 'Frazer is killed'—'Frazer is killed,' just as Father told it—to him."[20]

Dickinson wrote a poem about a Civil War soldier dying in battle on the banks of the Potomac River in Maryland. The soldier was from Amherst and Dickinson knew him and his family. His mother

The Eastern Union Army (pictured) during the American Civil War was also known as the Army of the Potomac. Many men from Amherst fought and were killed in the war. Dickinson wrote a poem, "Along the Banks of the Potomac," about one of them.

died when Dickinson was a girl. Now, she mourned both of them in an elegy.

When Dickinson's poems were being edited after her death, Mabel Loomis Todd and Thomas Wentworth Higginson gave this poem the title "Along the Potomac." The Potomac River marks the boundary between Virginia, Maryland, and Washington, D.C. Many soldiers were camped there. There were several battles in the area. Although the poem was written in wartime, its theme is not the battle. Instead, the poem is about death and how the soldier will meet his mother—who had died years before—in heaven.

When I was small, a woman died,
To-day her only boy
Went up from the Potomac,
His face all victory,

To look at her, how slowly
The seasons must have turned
Till bullets clipt an angle,
And he passed quickly round!
If pride shall be in Paradise
Ourself cannot decide;
Of their imperial conduct,
No person testified.

But proud in apparition
That woman and her boy
Pass back and forth before my brain,
As ever in the sky.[21]

Losing Sight

Dickinson's eyes began to give her trouble. Most likely, she was suffering from eye strain from writing all night. She described the pain in her eyes as an ache. Dickinson went to see Dr. Henry Williams in Boston in February 1864. She was treated from April to November of that year and could do very little reading or writing. Dickinson was also told to avoid bright light. Making plans to return home, she wrote that Vinnie should come and pick her up alone. "Let no one beside, come," Dickinson told her. "[I miss you most.]"[22]

Despite the trouble with her vision, Emily Dickinson would continued to write during the 1870s.

A LETTER TO THE WORLD

Thomas Higginson visited Emily Dickinson in Amherst in August 1870. Although he was hesitant to recommend that Dickinson publish her poems, Higginson was in awe of her creative spirit. He also found the family to be more independent than most. The household, he said, was a place "where each member runs his or her own selves."[1]

Dickinson was forty at the time, and Higginson described her as childlike and "a little plain woman with two smooth bands of reddish hair."[2] Dickinson wore a white-and-blue shawl and when she came into the room she dramatically handed him two lilies and said, "These are my introduction."[3] She asked him to forgive her for being nervous, but she never saw strangers. He forgave her entirely. She was, he said, "thoroughly ingenuous [innocent] & simple."[4] The two of them talked about books and poetry, and he came away feeling that she was someone who was unique and very special.

Higginson came to Amherst only one more time. In December 1873 he visited Amherst while on a lecture tour. (He gave a lecture on women's rights.) Describing his visit with Dickinson to his wife, he said: "She says, 'there is always one thing to be grateful for—that one is one's self & not somebody else.'"[5] But his initial impression of her stuck. Dickinson's intensity was marvelous, he said, but it "drained my nerve power so much."[6]

Although he remained impressed with Dickinson, Higginson did not really do anything to help her as a writer. "I hope you will not cease to trust me and turn to me; and I will try to speak the truth to you, and with love," he wrote Dickinson after their visit.[7] But he may have found her overwhelming as a person. He described her as his "eccentric poetess" who "*never* goes outside her father's grounds & sees only me & a few others."[8] Throughout their lives, Dickinson sent him fifty-two poems and twenty-one letters but never saw him again in person.

The "Inflater"

As Dickinson withdrew from society, Vinnie became Dickinson's connection to the outside world. Over the years, Vinnie became very protective of her older sister and the family's reputation. She once said, "Father believed; and mother loved; and Austin had Amherst; and I had the family to keep track of."[9] It was a role that consumed her. And what about Dickinson's role, according to Vinnie? "She had to think—she was the only one of us who had that to do," Vinnie said.[10]

Vinnie thought of herself as "the Inflater." She once said, "One by one the members of my household go down, and I must inflate them."[11] Vinnie inflated the family by defending them against anyone who might say something unkind about the Dickinsons. Vinnie was so protective and loyal that if she ever heard any negative gossip about the family, she would track down the person who said it and give that person a piece of her mind. "Vinnie is full of Wrath, and vicious as Saul toward the Holy Ghost, in whatever form," Dickinson wrote. "I heard her declaiming [making a speech] the other night, to a foe that called—and [I] sent Maggie [the maid] to part them."[12] In a letter to her friend Mrs. Holland, Dickinson wrote that Vinnie "is far more hurried than Presidential Candidates—I trust in more distinguished ways, for *they* have only the care of the Union, but Vinnie the Universe."[13]

During Amherst's fire of 1879, Vinnie took care of her older sister. Vinnie crept up to Dickinson's bed and said not to be alarmed, "It is only the fourth of July." Dickinson described it in a letter to her Norcross cousins. "I did not tell that I saw it, for I thought if she felt it best to deceive, it must be that it was."[14] Dickinson said she could hear buildings collapsing nearby, and that Vinnie's quiet comfort was something she would always remember and appreciate.

Without a Father, but With Gilbert

Dickinson's father resigned as treasurer of Amherst College in January 1872. In 1873, Austin took over that position, and he served as treasurer of the college until he died. Austin was becoming as prominent in Amherst as his father was. In 1874, Austin launched a campaign to beautify Amherst. He helped to plant trees and planned the First Congregational Church, which was built directly across the street from the Homestead. Austin and Sue Dickinson's family continued to grow. On August 1, 1875, Thomas Gilbert Dickinson, known as Gilbert, was born to Austin and Sue. He was, by all accounts, a gifted and creative child. His curiosity and sweet temperament endeared him to everyone he met.

In June 1874, Dickinson's father was in Boston, attending to business at the state legislature. In the midst of a speech on the House floor, he fainted and was taken to the Tremont House, a nearby hotel where he had been staying. He never regained consciousness and he died. The doctor said he had had a heart attack.

Unfortunately, no family was with him. Everyone was devastated by the news of his sudden death. Austin broke the news to the family. "We were eating our supper when Austin came in," Dickinson wrote. "He had a dispatch in his hand, and I saw by his face that we were all lost, though I did not know how."[15] The family was stunned by Edward Dickinson's death, and Emily never quite recovered from the news. "The world seemed coming to an end," Dickinson's niece Martha commented on the funeral.[16] During the funeral, Dickinson stayed up in her room with the door only slightly open so she could hear people coming by to offer condolences.

Dickinson's mother was unwell herself, and Austin was so shocked and depressed that Vinnie had to make all of the arrangements for their father's funeral. She was said to have met the sad occasion with grace. She tirelessly consoled the family and kept the house open so people could come by, day or night. So many people wished to pay their respects to Edward Dickinson that chairs and couches were brought over from Amherst College and arranged on the lawn.

Out of respect, all the shops and businesses in Amherst closed down on the day of Edward Dickinson's funeral. The *Amherst Record* reported that, "he will be even more respected and honored now that he is dead, and his character is more fully understood."[17] Samuel Bowles wrote Edward Dickinson's obituary for the *Springfield Republican*, saying that he "possessed . . . *the courage of his convictions. This was the essence of his life—this is his noblest bequest to his community and his state.*"[18]

Years later, Dickinson recalled her last moments with her father. For some strange reason, on the last afternoon they spent together, she wanted to stay in his company instead of going to her room. He seemed particularly pleased that she sat with him instead of retreating to her room. He said he did not want their time sitting quietly together to end, Dickinson explained in a letter to Higginson.[19] Her father's sentiment embarrassed her, and when Austin came over, she urged the two of them to go take a walk together. "His Heart was pure and terrible and I think no other like it exists," she told Higginson.[20]

Easing Burdens

One year later, Dickinson's mother was paralyzed by a stroke. Dickinson, along with the maid and Vinnie, took care of her. Caring for her mother helped ease Dickinson's grief over her father's death.

At this point in her life, Dickinson had lost many friends and family members to illness and old age. When Higginson's wife died in 1877, she knew just what to say. "Did she know she was leaving you? The Wilderness is new—to you—Master let me lead you," she wrote to him.[21] She enclosed a poem as a way of condolence. In the poem, Dickinson suggests that Higginson's wife is closer to him now in spirit than when she was alive.

Thinking of their own deaths, Emily Dickinson and her mother wrote out their wills in October 1875. Dickinson's mother left everything to her daughters. Dickinson gave everything to her sister, Vinnie, and made Vinnie the executor of her will. This meant that after Dickinson's death, Vinnie would have the final say in publishing her sister's poems.

The will was executed by Judge Otis Lord, of Salem. Judge Lord and his wife were friends of the Dickinson family. They often visited the Dickinsons. After his wife died, a romance blossomed between the judge and Dickinson, although he was several years older. "I confess that I love him—I rejoice that

I love him—I thank the Maker of Heaven and Earth—that gave him to me [to] love," Dickinson wrote in a draft letter to Judge Lord.[22] The relationship consumed Dickinson in a way that she had never been before. "Don't you know you have taken my Will away and I 'know not where' you 'have laid' it?"[23]

The Mysterious Master

In November 1875, Higginson gave a public reading of some of the poems Dickinson sent him. He was giving a talk about "Two Unknown Poetesses" at the Woman's Club in Boston, so he did not reveal her name. The "weird & strange power" of Dickinson's poems "excited much interest," he said later.[24] It is ironic that Higginson got such a strong reception for her poems. He corresponded with Dickinson, and the two shared books and insights, but he did not believe her poems were worth publishing because they were unconventionally written. The poems were not in a prescribed, classical format. Higginson even sometimes referred to Dickinson as his "partially cracked poetess."[25] Their correspondence is peppered with Dickinson's requests for him to continue writing to her. "Must I lose the Friend that saved my Life, without inquiring why?" she once asked him.[26] Though he may have been the mysterious "Master," their relationship was not an easy one.

Sue Dickinson had quietly spread a rumor that Dickinson's "Master" was the Reverend Charles Wadsworth. Samuel Bowles, the editor of the *Springfield Republican*, was also suspected as the mysterious "Master." He was a friend of Austin and Sue's, which is how Dickinson met him. He was very generous and compassionate. Some of Dickinson's poems allude to things they both read or wrote to each other about.[27] As an editor, Bowles had inside access to writers. He brought over manuscripts of famous writers for her to read. During their visits, he shared his impressions of the authors he met, including Charles Dickens.

Bowles was also one of the few people that Dickinson would still see after she retired from society. Around 1877, Bowles came to visit Dickinson, but she refused to see him. He was said to have shouted up the stairs: "Emily, you wretch! No more of this nonsense! I've traveled all the way from

Samuel Bowles was Dickinson's good friend and editor of the local paper, the Springfield Republican.

Springfield to see you. Come down at once!"[28] Dickinson came down and was pleasant and charming, as if nothing out of the ordinary had happened.

Austin's Confidante

Austin frowned on Sue's social gatherings. He often spent evenings with his sisters next door. His marriage was not a happy one.

In the fall of 1881, David Peck Todd and his wife Mabel Loomis Todd came to Amherst. David Todd was to teach astronomy at Amherst College. The couple lived near the Dickinsons, and within a short time became friends with Sue, Vinnie, and even (through her letters) Dickinson. At the time, relations between the two Dickinson households were strained. Strangely enough, Sue warned Mabel Todd not to visit Lavinia and Emily, and Lavinia warned Mabel Todd not to befriend Sue. But Todd became friends with each of the Dickinsons. Although Todd never met Dickinson in person, the two women communicated through notes and letters.

It was said that Austin and Sue's son, Ned Dickinson, who was only twenty at the time, fell in love with the charming and intelligent Todd. She left town for a while to try to let his affection for her dissipate. But when she returned three months later, Ned still had romantic feelings for her. Mabel

Pictured are the Amherst College grounds—including the observatory (right) where David Todd did his research.

was also well-liked by the rest of the Dickinson family.

Austin and Mabel began a close friendship in September 1882, which was to last until Austin's death and would greatly affect Dickinson. While their friendship tore the Dickinson family apart, without it, Mabel Todd might not have been so insistent on publishing Dickinson's poetry—or had such intimate access to Dickinson's poems after her death in 1884.

Both David Todd and Austin were employees of Amherst College, and Todd professed great respect for Austin. "My best friend died tonight, and I seem stranded," Todd wrote in his diary shortly after Austin died.[29] However, David Todd was said to be heartbroken over Austin's friendship with Mabel, although he tolerated it. But the friendship did take a toll on Todd. He spent his later days at a mental hospital, where he was said to weep uncontrollably whenever anyone mentioned the name "Dickinson."[30] Lavinia acted as a go-between for Mabel Todd and Austin. Lavinia would address envelopes in her handwriting so the two could pass letters back and forth, and she allowed them to meet at the Homestead.

It was this kind of intrigue that inspired Dickinson's writing. What better subjects for her poetry than the turmoil of the personal relationships around her? As she always did, Dickinson observed from a distance and told the truth—but told it in such a way as to ease the pain associated with the truth's hard edges. So she told the truth, but told it slant.

Pressures to Publish

In the summer of 1874, the "Saxe Holme" stories were published by Thomas Niles, a famous publisher in Boston. There was speculation at the time that Dickinson had secretly written the stories under a pseudonym, or fake name. Many of the local papers

Author and childhood friend Helen Hunt Jackson continuously urged Emily Dickinson to publish. She also fought the mistreatment of the American Indians.

were writing about the issue. But it became widely accepted that Helen Hunt Jackson had written them.[31] Helen Hunt Jackson had once been a schoolmate of Dickinson's and was a respected author and editor in her own right. Jackson wrote a book about the treatment of American Indians and was a friend of Thomas Wentworth Higginson. In fact, Higginson had helped Jackson's early writing career in ways that he was not willing or able to help Dickinson's.

Jackson wanted to publish Dickinson's poetry. In a letter to her, Jackson praised Dickinson and called her a great poet. "It is wrong to the day you live in, that you will not sing aloud," Jackson said. "When you are what men call dead, you will be sorry you were so stingy."[32] But Dickinson had allegedly told a friend, Clara Newman Turner, that she did not think it was "feminine" to publish.[33]

Jackson tried hard to convince Dickinson to

publish her poems in the "No Name Series," a collection of stories and poems to be edited by the Boston publisher Thomas Niles. The collection—like the title indicated—would be published anonymously, or without giving the authors' names, so Dickinson need not fear publicity. "Let somebody somewhere whom you do not know have the same pleasure in reading your poetry," Jackson urged.[34] While Dickinson stalled, Jackson persuaded. She would copy the verses in her own handwriting, Jackson said, and send them to the publisher herself so no one would know Dickinson wrote them. Clearly, Dickinson did want to be published. When Jackson visited Dickinson in October 1878, Dickinson actually came downstairs to talk with her. It was something she rarely did anymore. It is unclear whether Dickinson gave Jackson permission to publish her poetry. However, when *A Masque of Poets* was published later that year, Dickinson's poem, "Success," was included:

Success is counted sweetest
By those who ne'er succeed.
To comprehend a nectar
Requires sorest need.

Not one of all the purple host
Who took the flag to-day
Can tell the definition,
So clear, of victory,

As he, defeated, dying,
On whose forbidden ear
The distant strains of triumph
Break, agonized and clear.[35]

After "Success" was published, Dickinson began sending letters and poems to Thomas Niles. She sent him "My Cricket" and "Snow." Niles was very receptive, partly because Jackson had recommended Dickinson's poems so highly. "[Jackson] once told me that she wished you could be induced to publish a volume of poems," Niles wrote to Dickinson. "I should not want to say how highly she praised them, but to such an extent that I wish also that you could."[36] In response, Dickinson sent him another poem that implied that she was happy to remain anonymous and unpublished in the traditional sense:

How happy is the little stone
That rambles in the road alone,
And doesn't care about careers,
And exigencies never fears;
Whose coat of elemental brown
A passing universe put on;
And independent as the sun,
Associates or glows alone,
Fulfilling absolute decree
In casual simplicity.[37]

7

COUNTRY BURIALS

The last years of Dickinson's life were filled with care and sorrow. Dickinson spent a great deal of time caring for her mother, who had been unwell since her stroke in 1875. Dickinson's mother became totally dependent on her daughters. She could not walk and spent her last days moving from the bed to a chair in her room, back to bed—what Dickinson called her mother's "little Voyages."[1]

Mother and daughter had never been especially close. By all accounts, Dickinson's mother did not understand her daughter's perspective on life. But Dickinson explained that her tender feelings grew as she cared for her mother in her last illness. Dickinson wrote to Mrs. Holland, "We were never

The Dickinsons moved back to the Homestead in 1855. It was here that Emily Dickinson would spend the rest of her life.

intimate [Mother and Children] while she was our Mother—but Mines in the same ground meet by tunneling and when she became our Child, the Affection came."[2]

Dickinson's mother died in 1882. She probably died of complications from rheumatism, a disease that attacks the joints and makes them ache. "Only the Night before she died, she was happy and hungry and ate a little Supper," Dickinson wrote to Mrs. Holland. Her mother's death was, it seems, peaceful. "After a restless Night, complaining of great weariness, she was lifted earlier than usual from her Bed to her Chair, when a few quick breaths and a 'Don't leave me, Vinnie' and her sweet being closed."[3] Vinnie tended to the details of the funeral, calling it the "*last party* mother would give."[4] After her mother's death, Dickinson wrote, "Eternity. . . . sweeps around me like a sea."[5] Little did she realize at the time that another death loomed.

"Death of a Promising Boy"

Gilbert Dickinson, the youngest son of Austin and Sue Dickinson, died October 5, 1883. Gilbert was only eight years old and had been Dickinson's favorite. He was sick for only a week, but he could not fight off the illness, typhoid fever. The entire Dickinson family was devastated. Dickinson was at the Evergreens the night of Gilbert's death. It was the first time in fifteen years that she had been next door. She had stopped going to see people, and that included Sue, even though the two women still wrote notes and poems to each other.[6]

Gilbert was a precocious and intelligent child, much like Dickinson was at that age. He was perceptive and imaginative, and he and Dickinson shared a special bond. "Gilbert rejoiced in secrets. His life was panting with them," Dickinson wrote to Sue in an effort to console her. "I see him in the star and meet his sweet velocity in everything that flies."[7]

It was not just the family that mourned his death. Gilbert was such a delight that he made a lasting impression on the entire town of Amherst. His obituary in the *Amherst Record* was titled "Death of a Promising Boy." The obituary noted how the townspeople grieved for him. "When the village heard of his death we felt as if one had gone who had established a place for himself among us. We loved him."[8]

Once again, Vinnie was the strong one in the family. Austin was in such a state of mourning—much as he had been when their father died—that Vinnie was worried he would become ill himself. Dickinson grew ill after Gilbert's death and remained fragile for a long time. Vinnie wrote to friends that Gilbert was "the Child of the Regiment" and now that he was gone, she was having a hard time keeping the family together.[9]

Finding "a Treasure"

Judge Lord visited Dickinson frequently, and there may have been some talk of marriage—surprising after all her years of solitude. "The love I feel for you, I mean, your own for me a treasure I still keep,"[10] Dickinson wrote to him. The two had a similar perspective on life and nature.

Judge Lord held court in Salem, Massachusetts. Dickinson followed his trials by reading the paper. "Very sweet to know from Morn to Morn what you thought and said," she wrote to him while he presided over a murder trial.[11] Dickinson's letters to him brim with love and longing, and were surprisingly direct for someone who was constantly looking at things at a different angle. ["Oh, had I found it sooner!"] she wrote him of her feelings. "Tenderness has not a date—it comes—and overwhelms."[12] Judge Lord had been in ill health for some time. Shortly after the murder trial, he nearly died of a rheumatic attack. He did recover, much to Dickinson's delight. Tragically, Judge Lord became seriously ill and died of a stroke in March 1884. Dickinson mourned him and wrote an elegy for him.

The "Myth"

Emily Dickinson's own family perpetuated the myth of Dickinson as an odd person who avoided society. After her poems were published in the early 1890s, this perception of Dickinson flourished. She was portrayed as living a literary life of solitude, when in reality Dickinson's passionate verse reflected the turbulent lives around her. Mabel Todd never actually met Dickinson face-to-face, but she seemed to understand her. Shortly after her arrival in Amherst, Todd wrote to her parents of "a lady whom the people call the *Myth*. She is a sister of Mr. Dickinson, & seems to be the climax of all the family oddity."[13] Todd first heard Dickinson's poetry at Sue's house. Sue often shared the poems with other people. Sometimes she read them at parties, sometimes she enclosed them in letters she sent to friends. Todd wrote in her diary that Dickinson's poems were "strange" and "full of power."[14]

Emily Dickinson knew of Todd's friendship with Sue, Vinnie, and Austin and sent her flowers—hyacinths and heliotropes—along with a note: "Will Brother and Sister's dear friend accept my tardy devotion? . . . Please accept them now, with the retarded fervor quickened by delay."[15] Todd loved them, and she described the bouquet, as well as Dickinson's poems, to her parents. They were all, she said, "perfectly wonderful, and all the literary men are after her to have her writings published."[16]

Todd sent Dickinson a note and painted a flower on it. The two women struck up a correspondence. After Dickinson wrote her a thank-you, Todd painted her a picture of Indian pipe plants. In response, Dickinson sent her a poem: "A Route of Evanescence." Thus, their friendship began to take shape.

No Longer a "Nobody"

Dickinson had been getting more requests to publish her poems. She had been corresponding with Thomas Niles ever since *A Masque of Poets* was published. Around 1883, he began urging her to publish her poems. When Dickinson sent him some of her favorite poems written by the Brontë sisters, he said he wanted her original verses. "If I may presume to say so," Niles wrote, "I will take instead a M.S. [manuscript] collection of your poems, that is, if you want to give them to the world through the medium of a publisher."[17]

Dickinson flirted with the idea of publishing— she sent him "No Brigadier throughout the Year" (a poem about the blue jay, her favorite bird). A month later she sent him more poems, "The Wind begun to rock the Grass," "A Route of Evanescence," "Ample make this Bed," and "Her Losses make our Gains ashamed." The last poem was about the life of

At the Homestead in Amherst is a replica of Emily Dickinson's writing desk. Note the oil lamp that she used to write by at night.

Marian Evans, the famous British woman author who wrote under the name George Eliot. Niles had just published a biography of Evans and the poem was Dickinson's response to reading it.

Helen Hunt Jackson again wrote to her, practically begging that she be allowed to edit Dickinson's poems after she died. "What portfolios full of verse you must have!" Jackson wrote in the fall of 1884. "It is a cruel wrong to your 'day and generation' that you will not give them light.'"[18] But despite Jackson's pleas, Dickinson resisted this direct approach, much as she had throughout the years. She even wrote a poem indicating she would prefer to remain anonymous:

> *I'm nobody! Who are you?*
> *Are you nobody, too?*
> *Then there's a pair of us—don't tell!*
> *They'd banish us, you know.*
>
> *How dreary to be somebody!*
> *How public, like a frog*
> *To tell your name the livelong day*
> *To an admiring Bog!*[19]

Stopping for Death

Although Dickinson might have toyed with the idea of publishing, by 1884 her health was failing. She suffered from Bright's disease, an illness that affected her kidneys. Dickinson would stay in bed for months at a time, suffering from headaches, mild fever, and high blood pressure. Austin, despite being deeply involved in Amherst activities and with his law practice, frequently sat by her bedside. By now Dickinson saw no one but family—not even her doctor. The story goes that when her doctor, Dr. Bigelow, made his house call, Dickinson would walk by the doorway while the doctor sat in the room. He could not examine her or even get close to her. So Vinnie cared for Dickinson in her last illness just as she had throughout their lives.

Dickinson knew she was dying. She wrote notes to friends and family alike. She wrote to Higginson, telling him she had been quite ill, "bereft of Book and Thought."[20] To her cousins she simply wrote "Little Cousins, 'Called back.' Emily."[21]

One day in mid-May 1886, she went into convulsions. Austin described it as a "stark unconscious state." Dr. Bigelow treated her with chloroform and olive oil (hardly a cure by today's standards).[22] She remained unconscious, and the *Springfield Republican* reported her illness as fatal. Dickinson died two days later, on May 15, 1886, at the age of fifty-five. Austin described the day as awful. A grieving Vinnie told a friend, "How can I live without her? Ever since we were little girls we have been wonderfully dear to each other."[23]

This is the room where Emily Dickinson spent much of her later life.

As a token of respect for their lifelong friendship, Vinnie asked Sue to dress Dickinson and plan the funeral. Sue also wrote Dickinson's obituary that was published in the *Springfield Republican*. In the obituary, Sue tried to explain how Dickinson lived her life. Dickinson was simply being true to herself. Dickinson's seclusion was an intellectual choice. She was not "disappointed with the world," as some might believe, Sue said.[24]

Emily Elizabeth Dickinson was buried in Amherst on a sunny afternoon in May. Many people said it was beautiful in its simplicity. Higginson read one of Dickinson's favorite poems by Emily Brontë, "Immortality." Dickinson was dressed in a white gown and had violets arranged around her face. Friends said she looked peaceful and beautiful in her white casket. Although Dickinson had shunned people in life, Vinnie allowed people to look at her sister one last time before she was buried. Despite her age, Dickinson's hair was still auburn and her face remained unwrinkled.

Dickinson was carried out of the back door of the house—as she wished—through fields of buttercups to the Amherst cemetery. She was buried among a sea of flowers in a country burial that reflected the simplicity that was her outer life. The simplicity of her own funeral was reflected in a poem she wrote years earlier about the death of a friend:

Ample make this bed.
Make this bed with awe
In it wait till Judgment break
Excellent and fair
Be its mattress straight,
Be its pillow round
Let no sunrise, yellow noise
Interrupt this ground.[25]

8

LEGACY

Although she wrote about the subject of death in her poems, Dickinson once said she was horrified by the thought of death because the dead are "so soon forgotten. But when I die, they'll have to remember me."[1] More than one hundred years after her death, Emily Dickinson's words are more alive than ever, thanks to the preservation efforts of her friends and family. The Dickinson Homestead and the Evergreens next door in Amherst, Massachusetts, are historic landmarks and are operated by Dickinson's descendants. There is even a play about her life, titled, *The Belle of Amherst*.

During her lifetime, Emily Dickinson lived in her own unconventional way. In many ways, she did take the advice of Thoreau—to live deliberately. She chose to live deliberately—marveling in the wonder of nature and rejecting organized religion and marriage at a time when everyone expected her to embrace both of those things. Dickinson was, however, mystical and in tune with nature.

For decades, Dickinson saw only selected visitors but remained acutely aware of what was going on around her. She was a sensitive, intelligent woman with a quick wit and a fully developed sense of humor. Instead of interacting with people and doing

Emily Dickinson's gravestone reads "CALLED BACK." This was a quote from a letter she wrote to her cousins shortly before she died.

what society expected of her, Dickinson quietly continued to engage in her passion, writing. She withdrew if only so she was not distracted from her art. As Sue Dickinson explained in Dickinson's obituary, "Not disappointed with the world, not an invalid until within the last two years . . . the sacred quiet of her own home proved the fit atmosphere for her worth and work."[2]

Dickinson did not have to leave her house to find things to write about. While she lived in a small town, Amherst was hardly a quiet place. During her lifetime there were scandals galore: a minister who abused his children, burglaries, fires that devastated the town, an old woman who died and left everything to a young doctor on whom she had a romantic crush, the relationship of Austin and Mabel, and young college boys acting rowdy. She was surrounded by the deaths of her friends and relatives—adults and children alike. Dickinson observed all of this from a distance and told the truth of it in her own unique way.

Today, Dickinson's poetry is read on every continent. While she was once criticized for avoiding poetry's more classical structure, readers and scholars today are captivated by Dickinson's free-flowing verse. In fact, Dickinson is recognized as one of the first American poets to write in that "defiant" style.[3] Because of her crisp and imagistic writing style,

Dickinson is heralded as one of the first modern American poets. Her experiments with language are both emulated by poets and debated by scholars. The observation made by nineteenth-century New England editor William Dean Howells still stands today: "If nothing else had come out of our life but this strange poetry we should feel that in the work of Emily Dickinson America, or New England rather, had made a distinctive addition to the literature of the world."[4]

CHRONOLOGY

1828—Edward Dickinson and Emily Norcross marry May 6.

1829—William Austin Dickinson is born April 15.

1830—Emily Dickinson is born December 10.

1833—Lavinia Norcross Dickinson is born February 28.

1835—Edward Dickinson is named treasurer of Amherst College.

1840—The family moves from the Dickinson Homestead to a house on Pleasant Street in Amherst; Emily and Lavinia begin school at Amherst Academy.

1841—Edward Dickinson is elected to the state senate.

1842—Dickinson begins writing to her brother who is away at school; Edward Dickinson is reelected to the Massachusetts Senate.

1846—Dickinson begins writing to her friend, Abiah Palmer Root; Her schooling at Amherst Academy ends.

1847—Dickinson begins school at Mt. Holyoke Female Seminary in South Hadley, Massachusetts.

1850—Dickinson's valentine to George Gould is published in the Amherst College *Indicator*; Emily meets Susan Gilbert.

1851—Lavinia Dickinson begins writing a daily diary.

1852—Dickinson's valentine to William Howland is published in the *Springfield Republican*; Edward Dickinson is elected to the U.S. Congress.

1853—Austin Dickinson and Susan Gilbert are engaged to be married.

1854—The Dickinson family visits Washington, D.C.; Edward Dickinson loses his seat in Congress.

1855—The Dickinson family moves back to the Homestead.

1856—Austin Dickinson marries Susan Gilbert in Geneva, New York.

1858—Dickinson writes her first letters to "Master."

1859—Dickinson begins writing furiously and copying her poems into fascicles.

1861—"The May-Wine" is published May 4 in the *Springfield Republican.*

1862—Dickinson writes her first known letter to Thomas Wentworth Higginson on April 15.

1864—Dickinson spends several months in Boston receiving medical treatment for her eyes.

1866—"The Snake" is published February 14 in the *Springfield Republican.*

1870—Thomas Wentworth Higginson visits Dickinson in Amherst.

1872—Edward Dickinson resigns as treasurer of Amherst College.

1873—Thomas Wentworth Higginson meets Dickinson in Amherst for the last time on December 3; Austin Dickinson is elected treasurer of Amherst College.

1874—Edward Dickinson dies while in Boston.

1875—Higginson reads Dickinson's poems at the Women's Club in Boston on November 29.

1876—Helen Hunt Jackson asks Dickinson to contribute anonymously to a book of poetry; Jackson and Dickinson meet October 10; Dickinson refuses to contribute to Jackson's project.

1878—"Success" is included in Jackson's anthology, *A Masque of Poets*; There is speculation that Dickinson is a coauthor (along with Jackson) of the "Saxe Holme" stories.

1879—Dickinson begins writing to Thomas Niles, a publisher at Roberts Brothers in Boston; A great fire occurs in Amherst.

1882—Charles Wadsworth dies; Dickinson's mother, Emily Norcross Dickinson, dies.

1883—Thomas Niles of Roberts Brothers asks Dickinson to send him a volume of her poetry for publication; Dickinson sends him only a few poems.

1884—Dickinson becomes ill with a kidney ailment known as Bright's disease and never fully recovers.

1886—Dickinson dies May 15.

CHAPTER NOTES

Chapter 1. A Literary Treasure

1. Jay Leyda, *The Years and Hours of Emily Dickinson* (New Haven: Yale University Press, 1960), vol. 2, p. 482.

2. Richard B. Sewell, *The Life of Emily Dickinson* (New York: Farrar, Straus and Giroux, 1974), vol. 1, p. 221.

3. Ibid.

4. Mabel Loomis Todd and T. W. Higginson, eds., *Collected Poems of Emily Dickinson* (New York: Avenel Books, 1982) p. xix.

5. Ibid., p. xxi.

6. Ibid., p. xx.

7. Leyda, p. 473.

8. Todd, p. xxv.

9. Ibid.

10. Ibid.

11. Emily Dickinson, *Collected Poems* (New York: Barnes & Noble Books, 1993), p. 2.

Chapter 2. The Dickinson Heritage

1. Richard B. Sewell, *The Life of Emily Dickinson* (New York: Farrar, Straus and Giroux, 1974), vol. 1, p. 74.

2. Martha Dickinson Bianchi, *The Life and Letters of Emily Dickinson* (Boston: Houghton Mifflin Company, 1924), p. 6.

3. Thomas H. Johnson, ed., *Letters of Emily Dickinson* (Cambridge, Mass.: The Belknap Press of Harvard University Press, 1958), p. 404.

4. Jay Leyda, *The Years and Hours of Emily Dickinson* (New Haven: Yale University Press, 1960), vol. 1, p. 5.

5. Sewell, p. 49.

6. Bianchi, p. 10.

7. Millicent Todd Bingham, *Emily Dickinson's Home: Letters of Edward Dickinson and His Family* (New York: Harper, 1955), p. 25.

8. Sewell, p. 50.

9. Ibid., p. 78.

10. Leyda, vol. 1, p. 4.

11. Emily Dickinson, *Collected Poems* (New York: Barnes & Noble Books, 1993), p. 155.

12. Leyda, vol. 1, p. 42.

13. Mabel Loomis Todd and T.W. Higginson, eds., *Collected Poems of Emily Dickinson* (New York: Avenel Books, 1982), p. 36.

Chapter 3. School Days and Early Correspondence

1. Jay Leyda, *The Years and Hours of Emily Dickinson* (New Haven: Yale University Press, 1960), vol. 2, p. 477.

2. "Jane Eyre, an Overview," *The Victorian Web*, n.d., <http://65.107.211.206/Bronte/cBronte/eyreov.html> (December 10, 2002).

3. Alfred Habegger, *My Wars Are Laid Away in Books* (New York: Random House, 2001), p. 152.

4. Ibid.

5. Jay Leyda, *The Years and Hours of Emily Dickinson* (New Haven: Yale University Press, 1960), vol. 1, p. 119.

6. Richard B. Sewell, *The Life of Emily Dickinson* (New York: Farrar, Straus and Giroux, 1974), vol. 2, pp. 341–342.

7. Ibid., p. 341.

8. Mabel Loomis Todd and T. W. Higginson, eds., *Collected Poems of Emily Dickinson* (New York: Avenel Books, 1982), p. 206.

9. Leyda, vol. 1, p. 112.

10. Ibid.

11. Sewell, p. 341.

12. Thomas H. Johnson, ed., *Emily Dickinson, Selected Letters* (Cambridge, Mass.: The Belknap Press of Harvard University Press, 1971), p. 18.

13. Ibid., p. 19.

14. Leyda, vol. 1, p. 123.

15. Ibid., p. 125.

16. Sewell, pp. 344–345.

17. Edward Hitchcock, *Religious Lectures on Peculiar Phenomena in the Four Seasons* (Amherst, 1850), pp. 91–92.

18. Leyda, vol. 1, p. 130.

19. Martha Dickinson Bianchi, *The Life and Letters of Emily Dickinson* (Boston: Houghton Mifflin Company, 1924), p. 18.

20. Judith Farr, *The Passion of Emily Dickinson* (Boston: Harvard University Press, 1992), p. 2.

21. Leyda, vol. 2, p. 480.

22. Habegger, p. 221.

23. Farr, p. 251.

24. Habegger, p. 180.

25. Sewell, p. 142.

26. Ibid., p. 143.

27. Bianchi, p. 177.

28. Sewell, vol. 1, p. 163.

29. Ellen Louise Hart and Martha Nell Smith, eds., *Open Me Carefully: Emily Dickinson's Intimate Letters to Susan Huntington Dickinson* (Ashfield, Mass.: Paris Press, 1998), p. 7.

Chapter 4. The Writing Life

1. Emily Dickinson, *Collected Poems* (New York: Barnes & Noble Books, 1993), p. 253.

2. Jay Leyda, *The Years and Hours of Emily Dickinson* (New Haven: Yale University Press, 1960), vol. 1, p. 194.

3. Ellen Louise Hart and Martha Nell Smith, eds., *Open Me Carefully: Emily Dickinson's Intimate Letters to Susan Huntington Dickinson* (Ashfield, Mass.: Paris Press, 1998), p. 11.

4. Leyda, vol. 1, p. 212.

5. Ibid., p. 213.

6. Hart and Smith, p. 20.

7. Ibid., p. 10.

8. Martha Dickinson Bianchi, *The Life and Letters of Emily Dickinson* (Boston: Houghton Mifflin Company, 1924), p. 164.

9. Leyda, p. 197.

10. Bianchi, p. 173.

11. Ibid., p. 275.

12. R.W. Franklin, ed., *The Poems of Emily Dickinson, Reading Edition* (Cambridge, Mass.: The Belknap Press of Harvard University Press, 1999), p. 217.

13. Bianchi, p. 83.

14. Richard B. Sewell, *The Life of Emily Dickinson* (New York: Farrar, Straus and Giroux, 1974), vol. 1, p. 118.

15. Ibid., pp. 109–110.

16. Leyda, vol. 1, p. 207.

17. Sewell, p. 114.

18. Habegger, p. 373.

19. Hart and Smith, p. 76.

20. Sewell, pp. 131, 133.

21. Bianchi, p. 29.

22. Sewell, p. 143.

23. Hart and Smith, p. 21.

24. Leyda, vol. 2, p. 66.

25. Habegger, p. 324.

26. Ibid., p. 290.

27. Leyda, vol. 1, p. 233.

28. Michael F. Holt, *The Rise and Fall of the American Whig Party: Jacksonian Politics and the Onset of the Civil War* (New York: Oxford University Press, 1999), pp. ix–xiv.

29. Habegger, p. 296.

30. Ibid., pp. 328–330.

31. Ibid., p. 330.

32. Mabel Loomis Todd and T.W. Higginson, eds., *Collected Poems of Emily Dickinson* (New York: Avenel Books, 1982), p. 185.

Chapter 5. Strange to Some

1. Richard B. Sewell, *The Life of Emily Dickinson* (New York: Farrar, Straus and Giroux, 1974), vol. 2, p. 534.

2. Judith Farr, *The Passion of Emily Dickinson* (Cambridge, Mass.: Harvard University Press, 1992), p. 5.

3. "Hudson River School," *Hermes Fine Arts*, n.d., <http://www.hermus.com/hudson.htm> (December 10, 2002).

4. Sewell, p. 541.

5. Jay Leyda, *The Years and Hours of Emily Dickinson* (New Haven: Yale University Press, 1960), vol. 2, p. 56.

6. Sewell, p. 542.

7. Leyda, vol. 2, p. 63.

8. Ibid., pp. 60–61.

9. Sewell, vol. 1, p. 223.

10. Ibid., p. 134.

11. Leyda, vol. 2, p. 480.

12. Martha Dickinson Bianchi, *Emily Dickinson: Face to Face* (Boston: Houghton Mifflin Co., 1932), p. 66.

13. Emily Dickinson, *Collected Poems* (New York: Barnes & Noble Books, 1993), pp. 9–10.

14. Henry David Thoreau, *Walden* (New York: AMS Press, 1982), p. 1.

15. Ralph Waldo Emerson, *The Complete Works of Ralph Waldo Emerson* (Boston: Houghton Mifflin Co., 1903), p. 45.

16. Farr, p. 27.

17. Ibid., p. 189.

18. Mabel Loomis Todd and T.W. Higginson, eds., *Collected Poems of Emily Dickinson* (New York: Avenel Books, 1982), p. 140.

19. Alfred Habegger, *My Wars Are Laid Away in Books* (New York: Random House, 2001), p. 403.

20. Sewell, vol. 1, p. 124.

21. Emily Dickinson, *Collected Poems* (New York: Barnes & Noble Books, 1993) pp. 197–198.

22. Habegger, p. 487.

Chapter 6. A Letter to the World

1. Richard B. Sewell, *The Life of Emily Dickinson* (New York: Farrar, Straus, and Giroux, 1974), vol. 2, p. 563.

2. Alfred Habegger, *My Wars Are Laid Away in Books, the Life of Emily Dickinson* (New York: Random House, 2001), p. 523.

3. Sewell, p. 564.

4. Habegger, p. 523.

5. Sewell, p. 566.

6. Habegger, p. 524.

7. Jay Leyda, *The Years and Hours of Emily Dickinson* (New Haven: Yale University Press, 1960), vol. 2, p. 212.

8. Ibid., p. 213.

9. Millicent Todd Bingham, *Emily Dickinson's Home: Letters of Edward Dickinson and His Family* (New York: Dover Publications, Inc., 1967), p. 414.

10. Ibid.

11. Leyda, vol. 2, p. 273.

12. Bingham, p. 374.

13. Thomas H. Johnson and Theodora Ward, eds., *The Letters of Emily Dickinson* (Cambridge, Mass.: The Belknap Press of Harvard University Press, 1965), vol. 3, p. 676.

14. Ibid., vol. 2, p. 643.

15. Martha Dickinson Bianchi, *The Life and Letters of Emily Dickinson* (Boston: Houghton Mifflin Company, 1924), p. 84.

16. Martha Dickinson Bianchi, ed., *Emily Dickinson Face to Face* (Boston: Houghton Mifflin Company, 1932), p. 13.

17. Leyda, vol. 2, p. 224.

18. Ibid., pp. 224–225.

19. Thomas H. Johnson, ed., *Emily Dickinson, Selected Letters* (Cambridge, Mass.: The Belknap Press of Harvard University Press, 1971), p. 223.

20. Ibid.

21. Johnson and Ward, vol. 2, p. 590.

22. Millicent Todd Bingham, *Emily Dickinson: A Revelation* (New York: Harper and Brothers, Publishers, 1954), p. 77.

23. Ibid., p. 82.

24. Leyda, vol. 2, p. 239.

25. Johnson and Ward, vol. 2, p. 570.

26. Leyda, vol. 2, p. 315.

27. Judith Farr, *The Passion of Emily Dickinson* (Cambridge, Mass.: Harvard University Press, 1992), pp. 185–187.

28. Johnson and Ward, vol. 2, pp. 589–590.

29. Sewell, vol. 1, p. 179.

30. Farr, p. 130.

31. Sewell, vol. 1, p. 223.

32. Ibid., vol. 2, p. 580.

33. Farr, p. 11.

34. Sewell, vol. 2, p. 582.

35. Emily Dickinson, *Collected Poems* (New York: Barnes & Noble Books, 1993), p. 3.

36. Johnson and Ward, vol. 3, p. 579.

37. Dickinson, p. 97.

Chapter 7. Country Burials

1. Jay Leyda, *The Years and Hours of Emily Dickinson* (New Haven: Yale University Press, 1960), vol. 2, pp. 331–332.

2. Alfred Habegger, *My Wars Are Laid Away in Books, the Life of Emily Dickinson* (New York: Random House, 2001), p. 607.

3. Thomas H. Johnson, ed., *Emily Dickinson, Selected Letters* (Cambridge, Mass.: The Belknap Press of Harvard University Press, 1971), p. 286.

4. Leyda, vol. 2, p. 384.

5. Millicent Todd Bingham, *Emily Dickinson: A Revelation* (New York: Harper and Brothers, Publishers, 1954), p. 57.

6. Habegger, p. 616.

7. Martha Dickinson Bianchi, *The Life and Letters of Emily Dickinson* (Boston: Houghton Mifflin Company, 1924), p. 85.

8. *Amherst Record*, October 17, 1883.

9. Richard B. Sewell, *The Life of Emily Dickinson* (New York: Farrar, Straus and Giroux, 1974), vol. 1, p. 146.

10. Bingham, p. 89.

11. Leyda, vol. 2, p. 365.

12. Bingham, pp. 57–58.

13. Leyda, vol. 2, p. 357.

14. Ibid., p. 361.

15. Ibid.

16. Ibid.

17. Johnson, p. 287.

18. Mabel Loomis Todd and T. W. Higginson, eds., *Collected Poems of Emily Dickinson* (New York: Avenel Books, 1982), p. xxii.

19. Emily Dickinson, *Collected Poems* (New York: Barnes & Noble Books, 1993), p. 17.

20. Johnson, p. 329.

21. Ibid., p. 330.

22. Leyda, vol. 2, pp. 470–471.

23. Ibid.

24. Ellen Louise Hart and Martha Nell Smith, eds., *Open Me Carefully: Emily Dickinson's Intimate Letters to Susan Huntington Dickinson* (Ashfield, Mass.: Paris Press, 1998), p. xv.

25. Todd, p. 217.

Chapter 8. Legacy

1. Jay Leyda, *The Years and Hours of Emily Dickinson* (New Haven: Yale University Press, 1960), vol. 2, p. 481.

2. Ellen Louise Hart and Martha Nell Smith, eds., *Open Me Carefully: Emily Dickinson's Intimate Letters to Susan Huntington Dickinson* (Ashfield, Mass.: Paris Press, 1998), p. 266.

3. Christanne Miller, "Dickinson's Experiments in Language," *The Emily Dickinson Handbook*, eds. Gunrun Grabher, Roland Hagenbüchle, and Christanne Miller (Amherst, Mass.: The University of Massachusetts Press, 1998), p. 241.

4. Alfred Habegger, *My Wars Are Laid Away in Books, the Life of Emily Dickinson* (New York: Random House, 2001), p. 628.

GLOSSARY

abolitionist—A person who worked toward making slavery illegal.

allegory—An expression of life through fiction.

aubade—A song or poem about the dawn or the morning in general.

elegy—A poem about someone who has died.

euthanasia—The act of killing or permitting the death, of someone or something that is suffering, in a painless way as an act of mercy.

fascicle—One of the parts of a book or an intended book.

ironic—Containing the use of words to express something other than or opposite of the literal meaning.

mentor—One who guides a person in his or her field.

metaphor—A figure of speech where a word or phrase usually indicating one kind of object or idea is used in place of another to suggest a relation between them. For example: "blanket of snow."

recluse—One who withdraws from society.

simile—A figure of speech comparing two things that uses the word "like" or "as." For example: "The sidewalk is as hot as the sun."

trope—Figure of speech.

Further Reading

Dommermuth-Costa, Carol. *Emily Dickinson: Singular Poet*. Minneapolis, Minn.: The Lerner Publishing Group, 1998.

Greene, Carol. *Emily Dickinson: American Poet*. Danbury, Conn.: Children's Press, 1994.

McChesney, Sandra. *Emily Dickinson*. Broomall, Pa.: Chelsea House Publishers, 2002.

Steffens, Bradley. *Emily Dickinson*. Farmington Hills, Mich.: Gale Group, 1997.

Thayer, Bonita E. *Emily Dickinson*. Danbury, Conn.: Franklin Watts, 1990.

Winter, Jeanette. *Emily Dickinson's Letters to the World*. New York: Farrar Straus & Giroux, LLC., 2002.

Internet Addresses

Dickinson Electronic Archives. 2000. <http://www.iath. virginia.edu/dickinson/>.

The Dickinson Homestead: Home of Emily Dickinson. © August 2001. <http://www.dickinsonhomestead. org>.

"The Poetry of Emily Dickinson: Complete Poems of 1924." *Bartleby.com*. 2002. <http://www.bartleby. com/113>.

INDEX